NATIONAL TRUST

Book of
Cakes

NATIONAL TRUST
Book of Cakes

Linda Collister

National Trust

Published by National Trust Books
An imprint of HarperCollins Publishers, 1 London Bridge Street,
London SE1 9GF www.harpercollins.co.uk

HarperCollins Publishers, Macken House, 39/40 Mayor Street Upper,
Dublin 1, D01 C9W8, Ireland

First published 2024

© National Trust Books 2024
Text © Linda Collister
Illustrations © Louise Morgan

ISBN 978-0-00-864137-5

10 9 8 7 6 5 4 3 2 1

Contents

Introduction

What makes a cake a cake? For most of us it's a sweet, baked confection, often round, and our word 'cake' comes from *kaka*, an Old Norse word that is still used in Sweden – these days denoting a baked sweet treat. However, the cakes we know and love today have evolved from bread. Long before humans became proficient with cultivated yeast, soaked ground grains sweetened with honey and wild fruits were cooked over stones to form heavy, round cakes with thick crusts. A favourite cake of early Roman times seems to have been a dense barley-meal dough flavoured with pine nuts, raisins and sweet wine. Over time, bakers learnt to use barm – the foamy yeast mixture on the surface of fermenting beer – to ferment their doughs, and their bread-like cakes became lighter.

All sweet breads were eventually made this way. As new ingredients became available to bakers they were added to the mix. By the fourteenth century yeasted fruit cakes, enriched with fat and sweetened with honey or (very rarely) sugar along with expensive imported fruit and spices, were commonly made for celebrations. Indeed, Geoffrey Chaucer wrote of a massive sweet cake made for a festival using the equivalent of about 13kg of flour as well as spices, currants and honey. For the very wealthy, such cakes were status symbols.

By the middle of the seventeenth century treacle and sugar had replaced honey, and those with enough money could get chocolate and vanilla too. It seems the British have long had a sweet tooth. Lighter cakes that we would recognise as sponges, made by whisking and beating eggs and sugar (sometimes butter too), then working in the flour, were introduced into grand houses in Britain in the sixteenth century by Italian pastry cooks. It was laborious work: the flour had to be finely sieved to remove as much of the heavier bran as possible, and the sugar, sold in the form of tall, paper-wrapped cones, had to be grated and then sieved. Ovens were difficult to regulate. These cakes – raised by incorporating masses of tiny air bubbles when sieving – were thinner and crisper than modern sponges, and were often called biscuit cakes to distinguish them from the rich, yeast-risen fruit cakes. Recipes appeared in cookery books from 1615 and the new method of long-beaten mixtures eventually became so popular that they all but replaced yeast-risen cakes.

Luckily for our home cake bakers the invention of a chemical raising agent – baking powder – in the 1840s meant that both rich fruit cakes and light sponges could be made easily and quickly: no more tricky, slow-to-rise yeasted fruit cakes, or arm-numbing, time-consuming whisking. As more efficient ovens and cheaper supplies of the essentials (a range of fats, sugars, fine flours, spices and fruits) appeared throughout the nineteenth century, home-baked cakes became a much-loved teatime treat.

A host of favourite cakes are baked in the cafés of homes in the care of the National Trust. Some recipes are part of the history of the house or local area, and have been handed down to today's National Trust chefs. Others have been created more recently, inspired by the story of the house or by garden produce. New life is baked into old traditions to become edible history.

Recipe Notes

- All spoon measurements are level, unless specified otherwise.

- 1 teaspoon = 5ml; 1 tablespoon = 15ml.

- Eggs are always medium, free range.

- Butter is always unsalted.

- Milk is semi-skimmed or whole (full fat).

- (GF) denotes a gluten-free recipe.

- Citrus fruit zest is always from unwaxed fruit, organic if possible.

- Look for dark chocolate with around 70 per cent cocoa solids (unless specified in the recipe); supermarket own-brands are excellent value. Avoid 'chocolate flavour cake covering' as it doesn't taste or work as well as chocolate itself.

- Make sure nuts are as fresh as possible; the oils in them quickly turn rancid when they are exposed to air or warmth, so store opened packs in the freezer.

• Spices begin to lose their flavour, power and aroma once opened, so check use-by dates.

• Richer and denser cakes made with spices, and those with dried fruits, usually benefit from resting for a few days after baking, and before cutting, to allow the various flavours to develop and deepen. The fruit gradually releases moisture, giving a more mellow and better-tasting crumb as it ages.

• As a general rule of thumb, if you don't have any self-raising flour you can use 1 teaspoon of baking powder to every 100g of plain flour.

• Oven temperatures are for conventional ovens. If you use a fan oven you may need to reduce the temperature by 10–20°C.

• Vegan or dairy free: Malty Tea Loaf (page 22) and Quick and Easy Farmhouse Fruit Cake (page 61) can be made with either dairy butter or a plant-based alternative. Plant-based cream is fine when used as a filling, for example for the Chocolate Cherry Roll (page 128). Other recipes may behave differently when using plant-based products.

Good Things to Know

• Although you can make a cake just using your hands, a wooden spoon and a mixing bowl – and a cake tin – some recipes need an electric whisk or a stand mixer. You will need an oven for all but one of the cakes in this book.

• Before you start, read the recipe! Then get all your ingredients weighed and prepared before you begin.

• Kitchen scales are essential, along with measuring spoons: a 5ml teaspoon and a 15ml tablespoon are the most useful, always measured level. Smaller spoons to measure ½ teaspoon and ¼ teaspoon are useful too.

• Good-quality cake tins are readily available from larger supermarkets, and it is worth taking time to grease the insides and line (according to the recipe) with non-stick baking paper, even if the tin is labelled 'non-stick'.

• A large wire cooling rack is convenient, although you can also use a clean grill rack.

• An oven thermometer is a good investment as oven thermostats can be unreliable. You need to understand how your oven behaves – they are all a bit different – and to trust your knowledge and senses: the baking times given in this book are guidelines. Always preheat the oven so that it is the correct temperature when you are ready to bake.

• The temperature of the ingredients is important. Eggs should be at room temperature, not fridge cold. The fat – usually butter – should also be at room temperature unless otherwise specified, for example for cakes made by the rubbed-in method. For cakes made by the creamed or the all-in-one methods the butter should be soft but not runny or oily.

• To grease and base-line a sandwich tin, a square tin, springclip tin or Swiss roll tin you will need a little very soft melted butter (or plant butter) and non-stick baking paper. Check that the tin is clean, dry and room temperature, then lightly brush the base and sides, not forgetting the rim, with the melted fat (it will harden to form a more effective barrier than oil). Put the tin on the sheet of baking paper, draw around it and cut out the disc, square or rectangle. Press it neatly onto the base of the tin. You can also use pre-cut discs.

• To grease and line the base and sides of a springclip tin or deep round cake tin (usually for a rich fruit cake), brush the base and sides with melted fat. Cut two discs of baking paper slightly smaller than the base of the tin. Fold a sheet of baking paper in two to cut a double-thickness strip, long enough to go around the tin and wide enough to stand up about 5cm above the rim. Make a fold about 2.5cm deep along one long edge of this strip, then unfold and snip diagonally up to the fold line at 1cm intervals to resemble a thick fringe.

Press one paper disc onto the base of the tin, brush it lightly with more melted fat, then fit the strip around the inside of the tin so that the snipped fringe lies flat on the base and the rest of the strip is pressed onto the sides. There should be no gaps or creases. Brush around the fringe with more melted fat and then press the second paper disc on top so that the side strip is trapped at the base between the two discs. Brush the inside of the lined tin with a little more melted fat. You can also use ready-made cake-tin liners.

• To grease and line the base and two short sides (ends) of a loaf tin, brush the base, sides and rim with melted butter (or plant butter). Cut a strip of non-stick baking paper the width of the tin and long enough to cover the base and the two short sides, plus 4cm. This slight overhang will help you to lift out the cake after baking and prevent damaging delicate crusts before they have firmed up. Press the paper into the tin – the long sides will not be covered by the paper so check that the corners are well greased.

The 900g loaf tin I use measures 25 x 12.5 x 7cm; my 450g tin measures 19 x 12.5 x 7cm: these tins are widely available.

• To tell if your cake is cooked, first use your senses – does it look golden, does it smell 'toasty', is it starting to shrink back from the sides of the tin? For delicate cakes and most sponge mixtures the best test is to gently press the top of the sponge in the centre with your fingertip: if the sponge springs back into place then it is ready; if a slight dent remains in the sponge or it starts to sink then it needs a few more minutes' baking time. For richer, heavier cake mixtures such as fruit cakes and dense chocolate cakes, push a cocktail stick or fine metal cake tester into the centre of the cake. If it comes out clean, rather than damp with cake mix, then the cake is ready. Some recipes, such as brownies, need to be slightly underbaked, with a moist centre.

Ways to Make a Cake

You can make a cake in various ways: some are straightforward, others need a bit of skill. The recipes in this book are for home bakers who want to bake a good cake without a lot of fuss, and use the following methods:

Rubbed-in cake mixtures are the simplest. All you need are your hands and a mixing bowl: the Apricot Marzipan Squares (page 144), Rock Cakes (page 137) and Welsh Cakes (page 142) are made this way. Although this method makes fairly robust cakes with less fat and a coarser crumb than other methods, you can help to make the cakes light and crumbly by adding air to the mixture: sift the flour, along with any spices, raising agents and salt, into the mixing bowl. The butter must be cool and firm; this will make it easier to work than room-temperature or soft fat, which can turn the mixture oily. Cut the butter into small dice, add to the flour and briefly toss them around with your hand or a round-bladed knife until just coated in flour. With clean and dry hands, pick up a little of the butter and flour mixture using the fingertips and thumbs of both hands (avoid using your warmer palms). Lift your hands to the rim of the bowl and gently rub your fingers and thumbs together so that the lumps of fat are broken down and combined with the flour as they fall back down into the bowl (adding air). Keep doing this until the mixture looks like

coarse breadcrumbs (this can also be done by pulsing in a food processor). Quickly mix in the other dry ingredients – sugar, fruit, nuts – followed by the eggs and/or milk and combine everything to make a fairly stiff mixture.

Melted mixtures are also straightforward: you will need a saucepan large enough to hold all the ingredients, plus a wooden spoon. The traditional recipes for Sticky Gingerbread (page 37) and Parkin (page 94) are made this way, as the gentle heat makes the heavier ingredients easier to combine. Cut the butter into small dice and put it into the pan with the sugar and golden syrup, black treacle, or a liquid such as tea or fruit juice, then stir over a low heat until the butter has melted and the mixture is smooth and lump-free. Some recipes need the mixture to be simmered or boiled. Remove the pan from the heat and leave to cool until barely warm but still fluid before adding the beaten eggs (to avoid scrambling them) and the other ingredients. Cake mixtures made this way are often described as batters as they tend to be runnier than those made by the other methods, but they bake to make cakes with a tender and moist crumb.

All-in-one mixtures are the go-to cake recipes when you need speed, simplicity and reliability: all the ingredients are combined in one large bowl by beating with a wooden spoon or electric whisk or mixer. The Quick and Easy Farmhouse Fruit Cake (page 61), Fairy Cakes (page 139) and the Chocolate Celebration Cake (page 111) are made this way. For a light result it's best not to cut too many corners. Take the butter and eggs from the fridge about an hour beforehand so that they are at room temperature (although you can gently warm eggs by leaving them in a bowl of lukewarm water for 10 minutes, and soften diced butter for a few seconds in the microwave); this will help them to combine quickly. Sift the flour into the bowl together with any spices, cocoa powder, raising agents and salt (even with self-raising flour many recipes will add a little baking powder to help the mixture rise well). Add the sugar, the butter or oil, beaten eggs and any liquid (milk, fruit juice, coffee, alcohol). If you are not using a stand mixer, put the bowl on a damp cloth to prevent it wobbling around, then start beating everything together – fairly slowly, to begin with, to avoid a mess. Once all the dry ingredients have been incorporated, scrape down the sides of the bowl and beat for a couple of minutes at fast speed, just until the ingredients come together to make a smooth and creamy mixture. Don't be tempted to carry on beating as you want the baked cake to have an even, tender crumb.

Creamed mixtures are used for most of our classic and best-loved cakes, including Victoria Sandwich Cake (page 92), Coffee and Walnut Cake (page 88), Rich Fruit Celebration Cake (page 75) and Lemon Drizzle Cake (page 28). The ingredients need to be at room temperature to allow as much air as possible to be beaten in. Make sure the butter is soft but not runny or oily, and beat it for a couple of minutes in a mixing bowl with a wooden spoon or electric whisk or mixer until it has the creamy consistency of mayonnaise. Scrape down the sides of the bowl, then gradually beat in the sugar: caster sugar (white or golden/unrefined) is better than granulated sugar for light sponges as it quickly breaks down when beaten into the butter. Light and dark muscovado sugars are heavier and add colour and a richer taste: they are used for most dark fruit cakes for a good moist crumb. Icing sugar is rarely used

for sponge cakes as it breaks down too quickly to help form the structure. Keep beating the butter and sugar mixture, scraping down the sides of the bowl from time to time to incorporate all the mixture, until it is much lighter in colour and in texture – allow about 5 minutes by hand or 3 minutes with an electric mixer. Break the eggs into a small bowl and beat with a fork until broken up (this will help them to combine easily with the mixture). Gradually beat the eggs into the mixture, about a tablespoon at a time, beating thoroughly after each addition to incorporate as much air as possible into the mixture – this free ingredient will give the cake its signature 'spongey' texture. Add a tablespoon of the weighed flour with each of the last couple of additions of egg to prevent the mixture from splitting or curdling; however, it isn't a problem if it does start to separate or look bobbly as the cake will still taste fine, though it might rise just a little less. Sift the remaining flour (along with the salt and any spices, cocoa or raising agents) onto the mixture (this aeration will also add lightness). Gently fold in using a large metal spoon, turning over the mixture (rather than stirring or beating) just until you can no longer see any streaks of flour. Now fold in any extras – fruit, nuts, melted chocolate, liquids or other flavours as indicated in the recipe. A good test for the right consistency of a light sponge mixture is that it should be just soft enough to drop from a wooden spoon when gently shaken.

Whisked sponges are the most delicate of sponge cakes as they are raised entirely by air bubbles: the classic Swiss Roll (page 84, here flavoured with coffee), Blood Orange Poppyseed Cake (page 98), Lemon Cream Roll (page 100) and Chocolate Madeleines (page 150) are all whisked mixtures. Before the invention of baking powder, all sponge cakes were made by whisking eggs and sugar with a wire whisk for a very long time to form the necessary structure: the key to success is thorough whisking. Today, this calls for an electric hand whisk or a stand mixer with a whisk attachment. The eggs must be at room temperature, not chilled, so that they can be transformed with the addition of caster sugar into a cloud of billions of tiny air bubbles. Sponges made with whole eggs and sugar, called génoise or Swiss roll sponges, need whisking at high speed for about 5 minutes until the colour changes from bright yellow to a much paler creamy colour and the volume increases five-fold to a mousse-like foam. This mixture is ready when it passes the 'ribbon test' – a thick, distinct ribbon-like trail of mixture falls back into the bowl when the whisk is lifted from the mixture. Sift the flour (and any salt, cocoa or coffee) into the bowl and delicately fold in. Some recipes add a little melted and cooled butter at this point to make the sponge crumb a bit richer and moister (it will deflate the mixture slightly as it is folded in). Sponges where the egg yolks and whites are whisked separately with sugar, and then the light egg white meringue is folded into the mousse-like yolk mixture, along with the flour and then any melted butter, are called biscuit sponges; they are very light indeed, but robust enough to absorb a flavoured soaking liquid.

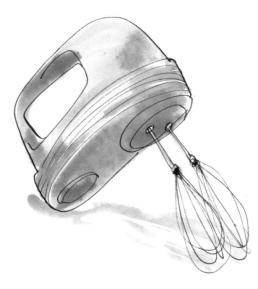

Loaf Cakes

Baked in loaf-shaped tins, these mixtures bridge the gap between yeasted breads and classic cakes: they are richer, sweeter and sturdier than a loaf of bread, but simpler and less elegant than a sponge or fruit cake. Tea breads, tea loaves and tea cakes, usually quickly put together, have long been a fixture on afternoon tea, high tea and supper tables across the country. Thickly sliced and often spread with butter, these robust cakes were sometimes known as travel cakes because they were easy to transport.

Bara Brith (page 41) is a good example of a bread that has become cakelike. These days it is packed with dried fruit and nuts, but it was originally made from leftover bread dough flavoured with fresh fruit – currants or blackberries – to keep the loaf moist for a couple of days.

Yeasted cakes were largely replaced in the mid-nineteenth century by simpler cakes made with chemical raising agents. In the right proportions, the combination of acid (cream of tartar) and alkali (bicarbonate of soda) produces tiny bubbles of carbon dioxide gas in a liquid mixture; they expand in the heat of the oven and are set in place as the cake mixture solidifies. Self-raising flour, with raising agents included, was invented in 1845 and was a huge success. Some older recipes call for a mixture of soured milk or yogurt with bicarbonate of soda to provide the lift. Avoid using more than the amount of bicarbonate of soda recommended in a recipe as too much of it can discolour the mixture and add a strange aftertaste.

The Sticky Gingerbread recipe on page 37 was regularly enjoyed by Queen Victoria and Prince Albert and their family at teatime as well as for grand shooting picnic luncheons. But the history of gingerbread extends back to medieval times, when it was made from a thick paste of rye flour or stale breadcrumbs, honey, ginger, cinnamon, pepper, nutmeg, mace and cloves, coloured with pounded saffron and pressed into elaborately carved wooden moulds. After baking, the dense cake was decorated to look like tooled leather and painted with gold leaf. This gave us 'gilding the gingerbread' as an idiom for excess. Described by Chaucer as 'roial spicerye of gyngebreed', it may have been our version of the *pain d'épices* recorded in Dijon, France, in the 1420s. As mustard is the only spice native to our shores, the lavish amounts of spices needed for these confections were imported at some cost. Ginger, originally from India, was widely used in medieval dishes. It was sold as the finely ground powder we know today or crystallised in sugar. Highly decorated gilded gingerbreads, some with elaborate removable almond-paste coverings, were still seen in the late eighteenth century, by which time the recipes had evolved: black treacle replaced the honey, wheat flour and eggs made the mixture lighter in texture, and melted butter or lard added richness. Parkin (page 94), a speciality of Northern England, similarly flavoured with ginger and black treacle or golden syrup, is a popular Bonfire Night treat.

Bananas, imported from the Canary Islands, were first seen in England in 1633 at Thomas Johnson's herbalist's shop in London. In the early nineteenth century, some enterprising British gardeners with specially designed glasshouses managed to cultivate banana plants, and when refrigerated ships began sailing at the start of the twentieth century the first London banana-ripening warehouses opened for business. At first bananas were a popular ingredient in savoury dishes. Imports stopped during the Second World War, but when rationing ended in the 1950s the fruit reappeared in abundance and banana bread soon became familiar.

Malty Tea Loaf

A simple, quickly assembled loaf cake made without eggs. It's based on easily available bran sticks breakfast cereal (such as All Bran; most are vegan but check the pack) and dried fruit soaked in spiced tea. For a vegan cake, use a good plant-based butter.

Serves 10–12

3 masala chai tea bags
500ml boiling water
70g unsalted butter (dairy or plant-based), at room temperature, diced
185g bran sticks cereal

275g dried mixed fruit
100g dried apricots, roughly chopped
140g golden caster sugar
185g self-raising flour
¼ tsp salt

Grease and line a 900g loaf tin (see page 12).

Put the tea bags into a large heatproof bowl, pour over the boiling water and stir well, then leave to infuse for 5 minutes.

Remove the tea bags, giving them a good squeeze, then add the butter, cereal, dried fruit, apricots and sugar to the tea in the bowl. Mix gently with a wooden spoon and leave to soak for 25 minutes.

Towards the end of this time preheat the oven to 180°C.

Add the flour and salt to the mixture and stir until thoroughly combined, then transfer to the prepared tin and spread evenly.

Bake for 55–65 minutes or until a cocktail stick pushed into the centre of the loaf comes out clean. Put the tin on a wire rack and leave until cold.

Lift the loaf out of the tin, wrap in foil and leave for a day before cutting into thick slices.

Date, Apple and Walnut Loaf Cake

Chopped dates soaked with honey and butter give this simply mixed cake a sticky toffee flavour. The first published recipe for a Date and Walnut Cake was in a *Woman's Weekly* magazine in 1939, and a pared-down version was popular during the war, when fruit replaced sugar in many recipes. This version is more luxurious, but extremely easy.

Serves 10–12

200g stoned soft dates, chopped
100g unsalted butter, at room
   temperature, diced
50g honey
150ml boiling water
½ tsp bicarbonate of soda
200g wholemeal plain flour

2 tsp baking powder
¼ tsp salt
1 tsp ground mixed spice
100g walnut pieces
1 eating apple, peeled, cored and
   diced
2 eggs, beaten

Grease and line a 900g loaf tin (see page 12).

Put the dates, butter and honey into a mixing bowl. Pour over the boiling water, then add the bicarbonate of soda and mix well with a wooden spoon. Leave to soak for 20 minutes. Meanwhile, preheat the oven to 180°C.

Sift the flour, baking powder, salt and mixed spice into a large mixing bowl, adding any flakes of bran left in the sieve to the bowl. Add the walnuts and apple pieces and mix in with the wooden spoon.

Stir the beaten eggs into the soaked date mixture, then add to the bowl with the flour mixture and mix thoroughly.

Transfer the mixture to the prepared tin and spread evenly. Tap the tin on the worktop to dislodge any air pockets, then bake for 55–60 minutes or until deep golden brown and a cocktail stick pushed into the centre of the cake comes out clean. Put the tin on a wire rack and leave until cold.

Lift the cake out of the tin. Ideally, wrap and leave for a day to allow the flavours to develop.

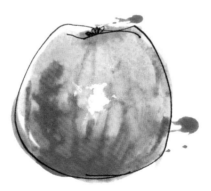

Elderflower Yogurt Cake (GF)

A quickly mixed loaf cake, with plenty of flavour from the elderflower cordial and lemons.

Serves 6–8

150g gluten-free plain white flour

2 tsp gluten-free baking powder

A good pinch of salt

50g ground almonds

175g caster sugar

Finely grated zest of 2 unwaxed
lemons

3 eggs, beaten

125ml Greek-style yogurt, at room
temperature

125ml light or mild olive oil

1½ tbsp elderflower cordial

For the glaze

100g icing sugar

Finely grated zest of 1 unwaxed
lemon

1 tbsp Greek-style yogurt

2 tsp elderflower cordial, or to taste

Grease and line a 450g loaf tin (see page 12). Preheat the oven to 180°C.

Put the flour, baking powder, salt, ground almonds and sugar into a mixing bowl. Add the lemon zest and mix thoroughly with a wooden spoon, then make a well in the centre.

Add the eggs, yogurt, oil and elderflower cordial and beat everything together with the wooden spoon until thoroughly combined and smooth.

Pour into the prepared tin and spread evenly. Bake for about 1 hour until deep golden brown and a cocktail stick pushed into the centre comes out clean.

Towards the end of the baking time, make the glaze: sift the icing sugar into a mixing bowl, then stir in the lemon zest, yogurt and elderflower cordial to make a smooth glaze with the consistency of double cream. If the mixture is too stiff, add more yogurt, a teaspoon at a time, or another teaspoon of elderflower cordial.

As soon as the cake is ready, put the tin on a wire rack and leave it to firm up for 5 minutes. Run a round-bladed knife around the inside of the tin to loosen the cake, then carefully lift it out of the tin and onto the wire rack. Put a plate under the rack to catch the drips, then spoon the glaze over the warm cake so that it covers the top and drips down the sides.

Leave the cake until cold before cutting into thick slices. Best eaten within a day or two of baking.

Lemon Drizzle Cake

Various polls confirm that Lemon Drizzle is our best-loved cake, but where does the recipe come from? Pound cakes, made from equal amounts of butter, sugar, flour and beaten eggs, became popular from the mid-seventeenth century, and by the 1820s finely shredded lemon peel was often added. The drizzle came later: in 1967 Evelyn Rose, a well-known Jewish food writer, published her recipe for a 'luscious lemon cake with a lemon syrup on top'. The pound cake recipe has evolved to a lighter, less rich mixture with plenty of lemons for that essential 'zing'.

Serves 10–12

220g golden caster sugar
Finely grated zest of 2 large
   unwaxed lemons
200g unsalted butter, softened
3 eggs, beaten
250g self-raising flour
A good pinch of salt

100ml milk, at room temperature

For the drizzle topping
Juice of 2 large lemons
About 100g golden caster sugar
  (see method)

Grease and line a 900g loaf tin (see page 12). Preheat the oven to 180°C.

Put the sugar and lemon zest into a mixing bowl and rub them together using your fingertips to release the fragrant oils. Add the butter and beat thoroughly until very light and creamy. Gradually beat in the eggs, beating well after each addition and adding a little of the flour with the last few additions to prevent the mixture from splitting.

Sift the remaining flour and the salt into the bowl, add the milk and gently fold everything together using a large metal spoon until thoroughly combined. Transfer the mixture to the prepared tin and spread evenly.

Bake for 50–55 minutes or until golden and a cocktail stick pushed into the centre of the cake comes out clean.

While the cake is baking, make the topping: measure the squeezed lemon juice, then weigh 10g sugar for every 10ml lemon juice. Stir together for a minute or so and then set aside until the cake is ready.

Put the tin on a wire rack, then gently prick holes all over the cake with a cocktail stick or cake tester. Drizzle the lemon syrup over the top of the cake so that it fills the holes (don't worry if it runs down the sides) and leave to cool completely.

Run a round-bladed knife around the inside of the tin to loosen the cake, then lift it out of the tin. Best eaten within a day or two of baking.

Banana and Toasted Pecan Loaf Cake

Toasted pecans and maple syrup, plus a touch of dark rum, transform everyday banana bread into a real treat. Stoneground wholemeal flour adds to the nutty flavour without making this moist cake too heavy.

Serves 10–12

75g pecan halves
125g unsalted butter, softened
100g light muscovado sugar
2 tbsp maple syrup
2 eggs
1 tbsp dark rum (optional)
225g stoneground wholemeal
  plain flour
¼ tsp salt
2 tsp baking powder
3–4 very ripe bananas, about
  300g peeled weight

For the topping
75g stoneground wholemeal
  plain flour
75g light muscovado sugar
75g unsalted butter, chilled and
  diced
1 tbsp maple syrup
25g pecan halves, coarsely chopped

Grease and line a 900g loaf tin (see page 12). Preheat the oven to 180°C.

Put the pecan halves into an ovenproof dish and toast in the oven until slightly darker and aromatic, about 6–8 minutes. Leave to cool, then chop coarsely. Set aside.

Beat the butter in a mixing bowl until creamy, then beat in the sugar and maple syrup. Scrape down the sides of the bowl, then beat for a couple of minutes until the mixture is lighter in colour and texture.

In a separate bowl, beat the eggs with the rum, if using, until just combined, and then gradually beat into the butter mixture, beating well after each addition. Add a little of the flour with the last few additions to prevent the mixture from splitting.

Sift the remaining flour, salt and baking powder into the bowl, adding any flakes of bran left in the sieve to the bowl, and gently stir in. Coarsely mash the bananas (leaving a few lumpy bits) and add to the bowl along with the toasted pecans. Mix everything together, then transfer to the prepared tin and spread evenly.

To make the topping: mix the flour and sugar together, then rub in the butter, using your fingertips, until the mixture looks like coarse breadcrumbs. Drizzle the maple syrup over the mixture, then mix in the nuts. Scatter over the cake mixture, then bake for about 1 hour or until a cocktail stick pushed into the centre of the cake comes out clean.

Put the tin on a wire rack and leave to cool completely before lifting out the cake.

Marmalade Stem Ginger Cake

Marmalade is associated with Dundee, which was once a major importer of Spanish citrus fruit; the family firm of Keiller made the preserve of bitter oranges and sugar a commercial success and a breakfast table staple. For a good Seville orange flavour choose a well-flavoured medium- or thick-cut marmalade, rather than a fine-shred, sweeter jelly type.

Serves 10–12

175g unsalted butter, softened
90g caster sugar
Finely grated zest and juice of
   1 large orange
3 eggs, beaten
200g self-raising flour
200g marmalade

¼ tsp salt
40g drained stem ginger, plus
   1 tbsp of the syrup

To finish
   About 1 tbsp ginger syrup for
   brushing

Grease and line a 900g loaf tin (see page 12). Preheat the oven to 180°C.

Put the butter into a mixing bowl with the sugar and orange zest. Beat thoroughly until very light and creamy.

Gradually beat in the eggs, beating well after each addition and adding a little of the flour with the last few additions to prevent the mixture from splitting.

Mix in the marmalade, then sift the remaining flour with the salt into the bowl and gently fold into the mixture along with 2 tablespoons of the orange juice (you won't need the rest).

Roughly chop the stem ginger into chunks the size of your little fingernail and mix in along with a tablespoon of the ginger syrup. Transfer the mixture to the prepared tin and spread evenly.

Bake for 45–50 minutes or until golden brown and a cocktail stick inserted into the centre of the cake comes out clean.

Put the tin on a wire rack and immediately brush the top of the hot cake with the ginger syrup, then leave to cool.

Run a round-bladed knife around the inside of the tin to loosen the cake, then lift out using the lining paper.

Chocolate Chilli Spice Cake

A dark and rich loaf cake flavoured with warm spices. It's a sturdy cake, good for picnics and lunch boxes, but it's also glamorous enough for a tea party.

Serves 10–12

120g dark chocolate (about
   70 per cent cocoa solids)
185g unsalted butter, softened
275g caster sugar
3 eggs, beaten
275g self-raising flour
¼ tsp salt
½ tsp baking powder
4 tbsp cocoa powder
¼–½ tsp cayenne pepper, to taste

1 tsp ground cinnamon
½ tsp ground mixed spice
100ml milk, at room temperature

For the topping
80g dark chocolate (about
   70 per cent cocoa solids)
50g unsalted butter, softened
Cayenne pepper (see recipe)
1 tbsp cocoa nibs (optional)

Grease and line a 900g loaf tin (see page 12). Preheat the oven to 180°C.

Chop the chocolate into evenly sized pieces and put into a heatproof bowl. Set over a pan of steaming hot but not boiling water; don't let the base of the bowl touch the water. Leave to melt; avoid stirring – just tilt the bowl and gently push any unmelted chocolate under the surface. Remove the bowl, stir gently until just smooth, then leave to cool.

Put the butter and sugar into a mixing bowl and beat thoroughly until light and creamy. Gradually beat in the eggs, beating well after each addition and adding a little of the flour with the last few additions to prevent the mixture from splitting. Stir in the cooled chocolate.

Sift the remaining flour, salt, baking powder, cocoa, cayenne pepper, cinnamon and mixed spice into the bowl. Pour in the milk and carefully mix everything together using a large metal spoon.

Transfer the mixture to the prepared tin and spread evenly. Bake for 50–60 minutes until firm to the touch and a cocktail stick pushed into the centre comes out clean.

Put the tin on a wire rack, run a round-bladed knife around the inside of the tin to loosen the cake, then leave to cool in the tin. Use the lining paper to lift the cake out of the tin.

To make the topping: break up and melt the chocolate as before, then remove the bowl from the heat and stir in the butter until smooth and glossy. Stir in a very small amount of cayenne pepper to taste – just enough to cover the tip of a sharp knife (don't use your fingers). Spoon the topping over the cake, letting it drip down the sides, then sprinkle with cocoa nibs, if using, and leave to firm up before cutting.

Ideally, keep for a day or so before cutting to allow the flavours to develop.

Sticky Gingerbread

This is a traditional dark and moist cake, rich with spices and black treacle. A close cousin of Parkin (page 94), it also gets better as it matures, so plan on baking at least four days before cutting.

Serves 10–12

115g black treacle
115g golden syrup
280ml milk
110g dark muscovado sugar
230g self-raising flour
¼ tsp salt
1 tsp bicarbonate of soda
1 tbsp ground ginger

1 tsp ground cinnamon
1 tsp ground mixed spice
¼ tsp ground cloves
A few grinds of black pepper
110g unsalted butter, chilled and diced
75g glacé ginger, finely chopped
1 egg, at room temperature

Grease and line a 900g loaf tin (see page 12). Preheat the oven to 180°C.

Weigh the treacle and syrup into a small pan and heat gently, stirring, until melted and smooth. Set aside until just warm but still fluid.

Meanwhile, gently heat the milk and sugar in another small pan, stirring until the sugar has dissolved, then set aside to cool.

Sift the flour, salt, bicarbonate of soda, ground ginger, cinnamon, mixed spice, cloves and black pepper into a mixing bowl. Add the butter and rub the mixture together using your fingertips until it looks like fine crumbs (alternatively, pulse the mixture in a food

processor, then transfer to a bowl). Stir in the chopped ginger, then make a well in the centre.

Mix the egg into the milk mixture, then add to the bowl with the treacle and syrup mixture. Mix thoroughly with a wooden spoon or wire whisk to make a thick batter. Pour into the prepared tin and bake for about 45 minutes or until a cocktail stick pushed into the centre of the loaf comes out clean.

Put the tin on a wire rack and leave until cold before turning out – the cake will sink as it cools. Wrap and keep for at least 4 days before cutting into thick slices.

Orange and Thyme Cake

A sticky cake rich in nuts, fruit and herbs from the café at
Ham House, a grand Stuart mansion on the banks of the
Thames in Richmond, Surrey. Built in 1610, it was extended
and transformed by the Duke and Duchess of Lauderdale,
courtiers to King Charles II. A painting at Ham House depicts
Charles II's gardener, John Rose, handing the King the first
pineapple to grow in the royal 'stove [hot] house'.

The seventeenth-century renovations included an Orangery
(now the café), a bake house, dairy, still room, icehouse and
bath house. The Duchess installed a set of walled gardens
producing cherries, apricots, soft fruits and vegetables for the
kitchens, along with orchards and an extensive herb garden;
herbs were used in the still room for medicines, as well as
in cooking.

Serves 10–12

---

3 oranges
1 tsp fresh thyme leaves
200g golden caster sugar
200g unsalted butter, softened
4 eggs, beaten
200g plain flour
100g ground almonds

2½ tsp baking powder
A good pinch of salt

For the topping
115ml squeezed orange juice
100g golden caster sugar
1 tsp fresh thyme leaves

Grease and line a 900g loaf tin (see page 12). Preheat the oven
to 180°C.

Finely grate the zest from the oranges into a mortar or heavy
bowl. Add the thyme leaves and 2 teaspoons of the sugar.

Pound them together to make a thick paste, using a pestle or the end of a rolling pin. Set aside. Halve the oranges, squeeze the juice and set it aside for the topping.

Put the remaining sugar and the butter into a mixing bowl or the bowl of a stand mixer and beat well until creamy. Scrape down the sides of the bowl and then beat in the orange zest and thyme paste, beating for a few minutes until the mixture is light and fluffy.

Scrape down the sides of the bowl. Gradually beat in the eggs, beating well after each addition and adding a tablespoon of the flour with each of the last two additions of egg to prevent the mixture from splitting.

Sift the remaining flour, the ground almonds, baking powder and salt into the bowl and gently fold in using a large metal spoon. Transfer the mixture to the prepared tin and spread evenly.

Bake for about 50 minutes until golden and firm when pressed in the centre.

Towards the end of the baking time, make the topping: put 115ml of the orange juice into a small pan with the sugar and heat gently, stirring until the sugar has dissolved. Bring to the boil and then simmer for 5 minutes to make a light syrup. Remove from the heat and add the thyme leaves.

Put the tin on a wire rack, then prick the cake all over with a cocktail stick and slowly spoon over the hot syrup. Leave until completely cold and the sponge has absorbed the syrup before removing from the tin.

Bara Brith

The name of this tea loaf from Wales means 'speckled bread'. There are two versions of Bara Brith: one made with yeast, the other with self-raising flour, but both use plenty of dried fruit. Penrhyn Castle in North Wales makes Bara Brith the 'quick' way, with self-raising flour, which would have been used in its Victorian kitchens. This version, made with yeast, includes cherries and walnuts along with the dried fruit, so it is very rich and has a really festive flavour. The loaves freeze well.

Serves 10–12

500g strong white bread flour, plus
extra for dusting
5g salt
7g sachet easy-blend dried yeast
1 tsp ground mixed spice
85g light muscovado sugar
450g dried mixed fruit

85g glacé morello cherries
85g walnut pieces
85g unsalted butter, melted
1 egg, at room temperature, beaten
About 165ml lukewarm water or
warm tea

Grease and line two x 450g loaf tins (see page 12).

Mix the flour with the salt, dried yeast, mixed spice and sugar in a large mixing bowl or the bowl of a stand mixer fitted with a dough hook. Stir in the dried fruit.

Halve the cherries, rinse with warm water to remove the sticky syrup, then pat dry. Chop roughly and add to the bowl. Lightly crush the walnut pieces with a rolling pin so that they are about the same size as the cherry halves. Add to the bowl, then mix until the fruit is well distributed. Make a well in the centre, then add the melted butter, the egg and 150ml of the water or tea.

Mix slowly, using your hand or the dough hook, to make a soft, slightly sticky, heavy dough, adding more liquid as needed. Check that there are no dry crumbs at the base of the bowl, then knead the dough in the bowl with your hand or the dough hook on the lowest speed for about 8 minutes or until the dough feels elastic.

Cover the bowl and leave in a warm place until the dough has doubled in size – about 1½–2 hours.

Punch down the risen dough to deflate it, then turn it out onto a lightly floured worktop and knead it for a few seconds. Divide the dough in half and shape each piece into a loaf shape to fit your tins. Gently press the loaves into the tins so that they fit neatly. Cover loosely and leave to rise as before until the dough just about fills the tins – about 1 hour.

When nearly ready to bake, preheat the oven to 200°C.

Uncover the tins and bake for about 35–40 minutes or until the turned-out loaves sound hollow when tapped underneath. Keep checking the loaves and be ready to cover with a sheet of baking paper if they start to look too brown.

Turn out and cool on a wire rack. Serve thickly sliced, with butter or cheese.

Fruit Cakes

Home-baked fruit cakes are part of our culinary heritage; we have good reason to be proud of our long history of baking rich and dark cakes packed with dried fruits, spices and nuts, along with plenty of butter, eggs and alcohol. Celebration means extravagance: special occasions, such as birthdays, weddings and seasonal festivities, require exceptional confections.

It still takes a bit of effort, along with a little practice, to bake a good fruit cake, plus plenty of time for the flavours to mature. We are so lucky today to have good ingredients readily available: just a few decades ago our grandparents needed to sort through the dried fruit, removing stones, stems and blemished items, before carefully washing and drying the fruit. Vine fruits dried to rock hardness needed to be soaked and plumped back to life with alcohol or cold black tea. Nuts had to be shelled and checked for freshness, then chopped or pounded by hand. For the best results whole spices were freshly ground, also by hand. Eggs were harder to come by in the autumn and winter months.

From the Middle Ages through to the nineteenth century, richly fruited cakes were made with barm (ale yeast) to prevent the crumb becoming a dense brick. A simpler version was the 'tipsy cake', basically a fruit-filled sourdough cake made with a fermented starter, fed and kept alive for the next cake (not easy in cold winters). It is still made in parts of Germany and by Amish communities in the USA. Eventually this hit-or-miss method was superseded by adding air and lightness to cake mixtures by beating – by hand. In 1769 Elizabeth Raffald recommended in her book *The Experienced English Housekeeper* that a cake mixture should be beaten for 2 hours, and that warm hands worked the best. Mrs Beeton, in her *Book of Household Management* (1861), advised replacing yeast with eggs, beaten for half an hour, suggesting that cakes made this way could be kept for longer.

The seventeenth century saw imported citrus fruits, chocolate and vanilla become more readily available, and these were added to recipes. Dundee Cake (page 72), made famous by the Keiller family, of marmalade fame, uses generous amounts of candied citrus peel. Fruit cakes soaked in brandy, covered in marzipan and hard white icing and elaborately decorated, became centrepieces for grand occasions and wedding banquets.

Baking powder, the cake-maker's saviour, along with more plentiful imported ingredients and better baking ovens, meant that by the end of the nineteenth century rich fruit cakes could be made easily enough to be regularly served by the well-to-do (who employed good cooks).

Though tastes evolve, fruit cakes are as popular today as they were 500 years ago. They have now become lighter and less sweet. From cakes made with fresh seasonal fruit, to the cut-and-come-again everyday fruit cake, or to specially made celebration cakes, these recipes still reign supreme on our tea tables.

Fresh Cherry Cake

A firmer, richer mixture than a regular creamed sponge is needed to support perfectly ripe, juicy fresh cherries. The flavour of this cake is best one or two days after baking.

Serves 6–8

250g fresh cherries, rinsed, stoned and halved
200g self-raising flour
175g unsalted butter, softened
175g golden caster sugar
3 eggs

A few drops of almond essence
50g ground almonds
A large pinch of salt
A large pinch of baking powder
50g flaked almonds
Icing sugar for dusting

Grease and line a 20cm round deep cake tin or springclip tin (see page 11). Preheat the oven to 170°C.

Put a third of the cherries in a bowl and set aside. Tip the remaining cherries into another bowl, sprinkle with a tablespoon of the flour and toss gently until just coated. Set aside.

Put the butter into a mixing bowl or the bowl of a stand mixer and beat well for a couple of minutes until very creamy, then gradually beat in the sugar. Scrape down the sides of the bowl and beat thoroughly for about 4 minutes until the mixture is light and fluffy.

Beat the eggs with the almond essence until just combined, then gradually beat into the creamed mixture, beating well after each addition and scraping down the sides of the bowl from time to time to incorporate all the ingredients. Add a tablespoon of the ground almonds with each of the last two additions of egg to prevent the mixture from splitting.

Sprinkle the remaining ground almonds over the mixture and fold in using a large metal spoon. Sift the remaining flour, the salt and baking powder into the bowl and gently but thoroughly fold in.

Add the floured cherries and any remaining flour in the bowl to the mixture along with half of the flaked almonds and fold in until evenly distributed. The mixture will be quite stiff.

Spoon the mixture into the prepared tin and spread evenly. Top with the reserved cherries and the remaining flaked almonds.

Bake for 60–70 minutes until the cake is a good golden brown and firm to the touch, and a cocktail stick pushed into the centre (avoiding a cherry) comes out clean.

Put the tin on a wire rack and leave until cold before turning out. Dust with icing sugar before serving.

Peach Melba Cake

This summertime recipe, developed by Lisa Hayes in collaboration with Dr Neil Watt at Mount Stewart, County Down, is inspired by the captivating painting *Circe and the Sirens* by Edmond Brock. Painted in 1925, Edith, Marchioness of Londonderry, is playfully mythologised as Circe the Sorceress from Homer's *Odyssey*. Standing in her exquisite formal gardens, surrounded by peaches – a symbol of immortality – she celebrates her triumph as a powerful woman able to transcend conventional boundaries to influence her world. This painting illustrates her horticultural success with delicate fruits and flowers growing in abundance in the mild microclimate of Strangford Lough, on the shores of which Mount Stewart stands.

Serves 10–12

200g unsalted butter, softened
220g caster sugar
3 eggs, beaten
125g plain flour
1½ tsp baking powder
A good pinch of salt
125g toasted hazelnuts, finely chopped

340g fresh peaches (about 2 medium), rinsed, halved and stoned
200g fresh raspberries
Icing sugar for dusting
Whipped cream to serve

Grease and base-line a 23cm springclip tin (see page 11). Preheat the oven to 180°C.

Beat the butter and sugar together until very light and creamy. Scrape down the sides of the bowl, then gradually beat in the eggs, beating well after each addition and adding a tablespoon of the flour with each of the last two additions to prevent the mixture from splitting.

Sift the remaining flour with the baking powder and salt into the bowl. Add the hazelnuts and carefully mix everything together using a large metal spoon. Transfer the mixture to the prepared tin and spread evenly.

Slice the peaches, then gently mix them with 150g of the raspberries. Carefully scatter the fruit on top of the sponge mixture so that it is evenly covered.

Bake for about 80–85 minutes until golden brown and firm when pressed in the centre – the fruit will sink into the sponge. Check for colour after 50 minutes and cover with foil if necessary to prevent the top becoming too dark before the mixture is fully baked.

Put the tin on a wire rack. Run a round-bladed knife around the inside of the tin to loosen the cake, then carefully unclip and leave until completely cold.

Decorate with the reserved raspberries and a dusting of icing sugar. Serve with whipped cream.

Fresh Apricot, Saffron and Honey Cake

The first apricot tree to be grown in England is believed to have been brought here from Italy in 1542 by Henry VIII's gardener. They are tricky to grow as they require a warm, temperate climate and a southern walled garden for success, such as the one at Ham House in Richmond, Surrey, which boasts a fine apricot tree. The ripe fruit are excellent when baked; in this rich sponge their sharp, intense taste is enhanced by the floral honey and saffron.

Serves 6–8

A large pinch of saffron strands
2 tbsp milk

For the apricot layer
About 20 whole blanched almonds
6–7 large apricots, rinsed, halved
    and stoned
45g unsalted butter, very soft
40g light muscovado sugar
20g honey

For the sponge
115g unsalted butter, softened
40g honey
85g caster sugar
2 eggs, beaten
65g plain flour
A good pinch of salt
1 tsp baking powder
65g ground almonds

Grease and base-line a 20cm cake tin or springclip tin (see page 11). Preheat the oven to 180°C. Put a baking tray into the oven to heat up.

Crumble the saffron into a small heatproof bowl, heat the milk until steaming hot and then pour over the saffron and mix well. Leave to soak.

To make the apricot layer: press an almond into the hollow in each half apricot. Mix the butter with the sugar and honey and spread over the base of the prepared tin. Arrange the apricot halves on top, cut side down, making sure they are quite tightly packed. Fill any gaps with almonds.

To make the sponge: beat the butter until creamy, then beat in the honey and sugar. Scrape down the sides of the bowl and beat thoroughly for several minutes until the mixture is light and fluffy. Gradually beat in the eggs, beating well after each addition and adding a tablespoon of the flour with each of the last two additions to prevent the mixture from splitting.

Sift the remaining flour, salt, baking powder and ground almonds into the bowl. Add the saffron milk mixture and carefully fold everything together using a large metal spoon.

Gently spoon the sponge mixture over the apricots in the tin to avoid dislodging the fruit, and spread it evenly. Put the tin on the hot baking tray in the oven and bake for 30–40 minutes until the sponge is golden and firm when gently pressed in the centre.

Put the tin on a wire rack and leave to cool. Run a round-bladed knife around the inside of the tin to loosen the cake and then carefully invert onto a serving plate.

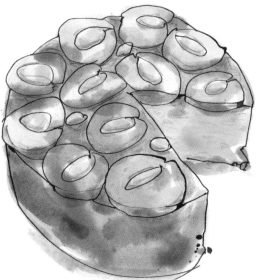

Pear and Ginger Cake

Just-ripe pears and fiery ginger are a wonderful combination for an autumn cake.

Serves 6–8

125g unsalted butter, softened
125g light muscovado sugar
2 tbsp honey
2 eggs, beaten
175g self-raising flour
¼ tsp salt
½ tsp baking powder

1 tbsp ground ginger
½ tsp ground cinnamon
30g glacé ginger, chopped
30g walnut pieces
2 tbsp natural unsweetened yogurt
2 just-ripe pears
1 tbsp honey, warmed, for brushing

Grease and base-line a 20cm springclip tin (see page 11). Preheat the oven to 180°C.

Put the butter, sugar and honey into a large mixing bowl and beat well for about 4 minutes, until very light in texture and colour. Scrape down the sides of the bowl and gradually beat in the eggs, beating well after each addition and adding a tablespoon of the flour with each of the last two additions of egg.

Sift the remaining flour, salt, baking powder, ground ginger and cinnamon into the bowl. Add the glacé ginger, walnuts and yogurt and gently mix everything together using a large metal spoon. Peel, quarter and core the pears, then cut into 1cm chunks and carefully mix in until thoroughly combined. Spoon into the prepared tin and spread evenly.

Bake for about 45 minutes or until a cocktail stick pushed into the centre of the cake comes out clean. Put the tin on a wire rack and immediately brush with warm honey. Run a round-bladed knife around the inside of the tin to loosen the cake, then carefully unclip and leave to cool.

Apricot, Cinnamon and Hazelnut Cake

Although they don't have the tart juiciness of fresh fruit, dried apricots are a handy store-cupboard standby for a well-flavoured, not-too-sweet fruit cake. The nuttiness of spelt flour works well with the lightly toasted hazelnuts.

Serves 6–8

75g blanched hazelnuts
140g golden caster sugar
Grated zest and juice of 1 orange
145g unsalted butter, softened
3 eggs, beaten
175g white spelt flour or plain flour

¼ tsp salt
1½ tsp baking powder
1 tsp ground cinnamon
140g soft-dried apricots, chopped
Icing sugar for dusting

Grease and base-line a 20cm springclip tin (see page 11). Preheat the oven to 170°C.

Weigh 40g of the hazelnuts into an ovenproof dish and toast in the oven until golden, about 5–6 minutes. Leave to cool, then chop fairly finely. Set aside. Halve the remaining hazelnuts and set aside for the topping.

Put the sugar and orange zest into a mixing bowl or the bowl of a stand mixer and rub them together using your fingertips to release the fragrant oils. Add the butter and beat well for 3–4 minutes, until light and creamy. Scrape down the sides of the bowl, then gradually beat in the eggs, beating well after each addition and adding a tablespoon of the flour with each of the last two additions to prevent the mixture from splitting.

Sift the remaining flour, salt, baking powder and ground cinnamon into the bowl and gently mix in using a large metal spoon. When thoroughly combined add the chopped toasted hazelnuts, apricots and 1 tablespoon of the orange juice. Carefully mix everything together; if the mixture feels stiff, stir in another tablespoon of juice – it should drop from the spoon when it is gently shaken.

Transfer the mixture to the prepared tin and spread evenly. Scatter the halved hazelnuts on top, then bake for about 50 minutes or until a cocktail stick pushed into the centre comes out clean.

Put the tin on a wire rack and leave to cool and firm up for 20 minutes before turning out. Leave until cold and then dust with icing sugar.

Blackberry and Apple Crumble Cake

Late summer brings a wealth of produce: slightly tart blackberries picked from the hedgerows and windfall apples not quite good enough for the fruit bowl make an excellent topping for a simple spiced sponge.

Serves 6–8

150g blackberries
2 eating apples

½ tsp ground cinnamon
¼ tsp grated nutmeg

For the sponge
125g unsalted butter, softened
125g golden caster sugar
2 eggs, beaten
125g self-raising flour
1 tsp ground ginger

For the crumble topping
50g plain flour
1 tsp ground ginger
30g golden caster sugar
35g unsalted butter, melted
Icing sugar for dusting

Grease and base-line a 20cm springclip tin (see page 11). Preheat the oven to 180°C.

Gently wipe the blackberries to remove any dust. Peel, core and thinly slice the apples, and keep separate from the blackberries.

To make the sponge: put the butter into a mixing bowl or the bowl of a stand mixer and beat for a couple of minutes, then beat in the sugar. Scrape down the sides of the bowl and beat for a few minutes until the mixture is lighter in colour and texture.

Gradually beat in the eggs, beating well after each addition and adding a tablespoon of flour with the last couple of additions of egg to prevent the mixture from splitting.

Sift the remaining flour and all the spices into the bowl and gently fold in using a large metal spoon.

Transfer the mixture to the prepared tin and spread evenly. Scatter the blackberries on top, then cover with the apple slices, making sure they are evenly distributed.

To make the crumble topping: mix the flour, ginger and sugar in a small bowl, then add the melted butter and work everything together, pinching with your fingers until the mixture looks like small peas.

Scatter the crumble evenly over the apple slices, then bake for 55–60 minutes until golden and a cocktail stick pushed into the centre of the cake (avoiding a blackberry if possible), comes out clean. If there is damp mixture clinging to the cocktail stick, return the cake to the oven for a few more minutes.

Put the tin on a wire rack and leave to cool and firm up for 10 minutes. Run a round-bladed knife around the inside of the tin to loosen the cake, then carefully unclip and leave to cool completely.

Dust with icing sugar before serving.

Best eaten within a day or two of baking.

Orchard Figgy Cake

An unusual recipe that is good for using windfall apples,
those slightly past their best, or just miscellaneous 'irregulars'.
It's inspired by Isaac Newton's orchard at his family home,
Woolsthorpe Manor in Lincolnshire. An apple falling from
the Flower of Kent tree he was sitting under formed the basis
of his theory of gravity. The ancient tree is still there,
producing apples.

   Here, a light whisked sponge mixture is packed with
sliced apples and dried figs, and finished with a crunchy flaked-
almond topping.

Serves 6–8

---

7 eating apples	100g self-raising flour
Finely grated zest and juice of	A good pinch of salt
1 large unwaxed lemon	
85g dried figs, chopped	*For the topping*
50g unsalted butter	15g light muscovado sugar
100g light muscovado sugar	1 tsp ground cinnamon
2 eggs	25g flaked almonds

Grease and base-line a 20cm springclip tin (see page 11). Preheat
the oven to 180°C.

Peel, core and thinly slice the apples into a mixing bowl. Add
the lemon zest and juice and the figs, then stir until thoroughly
combined. Set aside.

Melt the butter in a small pan over a low heat and leave to gently bubble for 2–3 minutes until it turns golden and has a warm, nutty smell. Leave to cool.

Put the sugar and eggs into the bowl of a stand mixer and whisk on high speed for 3–4 minutes until very thick and light. Gradually whisk in the melted butter. Sift the flour and salt into the bowl and fold in using a large metal spoon, then fold in the fruit mixture, along with any liquid left in the bowl. When just combined (avoid over-mixing), spoon the mixture into the prepared tin and spread evenly.

Combine the topping ingredients and scatter over the cake mixture, then bake for 50–55 minutes or until golden and a cocktail stick pushed into the centre of the cake comes out clean.

Put the tin on a wire rack and run a round-bladed knife around the inside of the tin to loosen the cake. Leave to cool completely before unclipping.

Best eaten on the day of baking or the next day, gently warmed.

Quick and Easy Farmhouse Fruit Cake

A simple all-in-one recipe, where everything is combined in a saucepan and mixed with a wooden spoon. The fruity mixture is flavoured with strong black tea and nutty wholemeal flour. It's lower in sugar and fat than most fruit cakes, and you can replace the unsalted butter with a plant-based alternative for a dairy-free recipe. The mixture can be made nut-free and finished with a sprinkling of demerara sugar.

Serves 6–8

350g dried mixed fruit (raisins, currants, sultanas)
250ml strong black tea
120g unsalted butter (dairy or plant-based), diced
100g light muscovado sugar
2 tsp ground mixed spice
225g wholemeal plain flour

¼ tsp salt
2½ tsp baking powder
2 eggs, beaten
2 tbsp flaked almonds (optional)

To finish
1–2 tbsp flaked almonds or demerara sugar

Grease and line a 20cm springclip tin (see page 11).

Weigh the dried fruit into a saucepan large enough to hold all the ingredients, then add the tea, butter, sugar and mixed spice. Put the pan over a fairly low heat and stir gently with a wooden spoon until the butter has melted. Turn up the heat and let the ingredients simmer for a couple of minutes, then remove from the heat.

Leave to cool for 15–20 minutes or until the mixture feels comfortable if you dip in a finger. Meanwhile, preheat the oven to 180°C.

Sift the flour, salt and baking powder into the barely warm mixture. If any bran fibre from the flour is left in the sieve add this to the pan too. Add the eggs and almonds, if using, then mix everything together with a wooden spoon.

Transfer the mixture to the prepared tin and spread evenly. Tap the tin on the worktop to dislodge any air pockets, then scatter the flaked almonds or sugar over the cake.

Bake for 30–35 minutes until a good golden brown and a cocktail stick pushed into the centre of the cake comes out clean.

Put the tin on a wire rack and leave until cold before turning out. Ideally, wrap and keep for a day or two before cutting.

Churchill's Fruit Cake

This excellent fruit cake, not particularly heavy or richly sweet, is inspired by one from Chartwell, the well-loved family home in Kent purchased by Sir Winston Churchill in 1922. The cake was a favourite of his, baked for him by his long-standing cook Georgina Landemare at 10 Downing Street during the Second World War when he served as Prime Minister, and later at Chartwell. In 1966, following his death the previous year, the house, still filled with his treasures, was opened to the public, having been given to the National Trust long before.

This recipe proved very popular when the Trust shared it as part of its VE Day anniversary celebrations in 2020, during the first Covid lockdown.

Serves 10–12

280g dried mixed fruit
200ml strong black tea, at room
    temperature
225g unsalted butter, softened
170g dark muscovado sugar
1 tbsp black treacle

5 eggs, beaten
285g self-raising flour
110g glacé morello cherries, halved
1 tsp ground mixed spice
Caster sugar for dusting

Put the dried fruit and tea into a large bowl, stir well, then cover and leave to soak for several hours, preferably overnight.

When ready to bake, grease and line a 23cm springclip tin (see page 11). Preheat the oven to 150°C.

Drain the fruit thoroughly, reserving the soaking liquid.

Put the butter into a mixing bowl or the bowl of a stand mixer and beat well until creamy. Beat in the sugar and black treacle, beating thoroughly until paler in colour and lighter in texture, regularly scraping down the sides of the bowl to incorporate all the ingredients. Gradually beat in the eggs, beating well after each addition and adding a little of the flour with the last few additions to prevent the mixture from splitting.

Rinse the glacé cherries if necessary to remove any excess sticky syrup, pat dry, then toss in a tablespoon of the flour and set aside.

Sift the remaining flour and the mixed spice into the bowl and gently fold in using a large metal spoon. When you can no longer see any streaks of flour, add the cherries and any remaining flour, along with the drained dried fruit. Mix everything together, adding a tablespoon of the fruit soaking liquid if the mixture feels very stiff – it should drop from the spoon when gently tapped on the side of the bowl – but it may not be necessary.

Spoon into the prepared tin and spread evenly. Tap the tin on the worktop to settle the mixture, then bake for 1½–2 hours. To test if the cake is ready, push a cocktail stick into the centre; if it comes out clean then it is cooked.

Put the tin on a wire rack and leave until cold before turning out. Wrap in foil and leave for a day or two before serving, lightly dusted with caster sugar.

Chocolate, Fruit and Nut Celebration Cake

A glamorous alternative to a traditional white-iced Christmas cake. The flavour develops as the cake matures, so plan on baking several days in advance of the celebration.

Serves 10–12

200g blanched hazelnuts
100g walnut pieces
100g shelled unsalted pistachios
250g unsalted butter, softened
250g caster sugar
4 eggs, beaten
100g self-raising flour
¼ tsp salt
100g dark chocolate (about 70 per cent cocoa solids), finely chopped, or dark chocolate chips

50g soft-dried cherries
1 tbsp hazelnut liqueur, cherry brandy or brandy

To finish
125g dark chocolate (about 70 per cent cocoa solids)
100g unsalted butter, softened
1 tbsp hazelnut liqueur, cherry brandy or brandy
Blanched hazelnuts

Grease and line a 23cm springclip tin (see page 11). Preheat the oven to 170°C.

Tip the hazelnuts into an ovenproof dish, the walnuts into another and the pistachios into a third. Toast the nuts in the oven until lightly coloured, about 8–10 minutes, but watch carefully as they colour at different rates. Leave to cool. Put the hazelnuts into a food processor and chop to small pea-sized pieces. Add the walnuts and pistachios and pulse for a few seconds to roughly chop these nuts too – you don't want them too small. Set aside.

Put the butter into a mixing bowl or the bowl of a stand mixer and beat for a minute until creamy, then beat in the sugar. Scrape down the sides of the bowl and beat on high speed for about 4 minutes until very light in texture and colour. Scrape down the sides of the bowl again and gradually beat in the eggs, beating well after each addition and adding a tablespoon of the flour with each of the last two additions to prevent the mixture from splitting.

Sift the remaining flour and salt into the bowl. Add the nut mixture, the chocolate, the cherries and the liqueur or brandy. Mix everything together using a large metal spoon, then transfer to the prepared tin and spread evenly.

Bake for 60–70 minutes until firm to the touch. Put the tin on a wire rack and leave until cold before turning out.

To finish the cake: chop the chocolate into evenly sized pieces and gently melt in a heatproof bowl set over a pan of steaming hot but not boiling water; don't let the base of the bowl touch the water. Avoid stirring; just tilt the bowl and gently press any unmelted chocolate under the surface.

Remove the bowl from the pan, add the butter and liqueur or brandy and gently stir until smooth. Leave to cool until thickened but still fluid, then spread over the top and sides of the cake. Decorate with nuts before the chocolate sets.

Leave overnight, or several days if possible, before cutting.

Kentish Ale Fruit Cake

The key ingredient in this recipe is the National Trust's own Kentish Red Ale; the hops (Kent Target and Goldings) are picked and dried at the Trust's last working traditional hop farm, Little Scotney, at Scotney Castle in Lamberhurst, and used in locally brewed craft beers. The ale, used to soak the dried fruit overnight, adds balance and a malty, toasted nuttiness that becomes more apparent as the cake matures, so plan on baking several days in advance.

Serves 6–8

500g dried mixed fruit (raisins, sultanas, currants)
100ml Kentish Red Ale (or other hoppy red ale)
100g walnut pieces
225g unsalted butter, softened

225g light muscovado sugar
4 eggs, beaten
300g plain flour
½ tsp baking powder
¼ tsp salt
1½ tsp ground mixed spice

Put the dried fruit and ale into a large bowl, stir well, then cover and leave to soak overnight.

When ready to bake, grease and line a 20cm springclip tin (see page 11). Preheat the oven to 180°C.

Put the walnut pieces into an ovenproof dish and toast in the oven until lightly coloured, about 8 minutes. Leave to cool. Reduce the oven temperature to 170°C.

Put the butter into a mixing bowl or the bowl of a stand mixer and beat well until creamy. Gradually beat in the sugar, then scrape down the sides of the bowl and beat the mixture thoroughly for about 5 minutes until lighter in colour and texture.

Scrape down the sides of the bowl again and gradually beat in the eggs, beating well after each addition and adding a tablespoon of the flour with the last couple of additions to prevent the mixture from splitting.

Sift the remaining flour, baking powder, salt and mixed spice onto the mixture and gently fold in using a large metal spoon. When thoroughly combined add the walnuts and the soaked fruit with any liquid left in the bowl, and mix everything together.

Spoon the mixture into the prepared tin and spread evenly. Tap the tin on the worktop to settle the mixture and then bake for 1 hour. Reduce the oven temperature to 150°C and bake for a further 50–60 minutes or until a cocktail stick pushed into the centre of the cake comes out clean.

Put the tin on a wire rack and leave until cold before turning out. Wrap and keep for 3–4 days before cutting.

Great Train Fruit Cake

Queen Victoria was the first monarch to use the train for regular travel around the country. The great expansion of the railways led to the opening of the world's first railway hotel, at Euston station, London, in 1839. For well-to-do travellers it was an oasis of luxury, with ornate furniture and excellent, substantial meals. The chefs, many trained in great country houses and grand French hotel kitchens, also supplied the trains' first-class dining carriages. This undecorated light fruit cake, with a thin layer of marzipan running through its centre, dates from those times.

Serves 6–8

175g unsalted butter, softened
175g light muscovado sugar
4 eggs, beaten
225g plain flour
1½ tsp baking powder
¼ tsp salt
70g ground almonds
450g luxury dried fruit mixture
  (including raisins, sultanas,
  currants, glacé cherries, mixed
  peel, diced dried apricots, etc.)
or 350g dried mixed fruit and
  chopped peel plus 100g glacé
  morello cherries, halved
About 2 tbsp milk
225g white marzipan
50g flaked almonds

Grease and line a 20cm round deep cake tin (see page 11). Preheat the oven to 180°C.

Put the butter into a large mixing bowl or the bowl of a stand mixer and beat until creamy. Beat in the sugar, then scrape down the sides of the bowl and beat well until the mixture is light and fluffy.

Scrape down the sides of the bowl again and gradually beat in the eggs, beating well after each addition and adding a tablespoon of the flour with each of the last two additions to prevent the mixture from splitting.

Sift the remaining flour, baking powder, salt and ground almonds into the bowl and carefully fold in using a large metal spoon. When thoroughly combined fold in the dried fruit and enough milk to make a mixture that just falls from the spoon when gently tapped.

Spoon half the mixture into the prepared tin and level the surface. Roll out the marzipan to a disc that fits inside the tin and gently set it on top of the cake mixture. Spoon the remaining mixture on top, smooth the surface and then make a slight hollow in the centre to help the cake rise evenly.

Scatter with the flaked almonds, then bake for 30 minutes. Reduce the oven temperature to 170°C and bake for a further 1¼–1½ hours or until a cocktail stick pushed into the centre of the cake just down to the marzipan layer comes out clean (the marzipan will be soft and sticky).

Put the tin on a wire rack and leave until cold before turning out. Wrap and keep for at least 4 days before cutting.

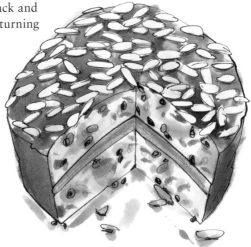

Dundee Cake

A rich fruit cake made with dried vine fruits, almonds, plenty of candied citrus peel and fresh lemon zest, but no spices. Dundee has long had a reputation for baking luxurious cakes: expensive fruits and sugar, along with nuts and citrus fruit from Spain, arrived at the port, and candied peel was a feature of cakes baked at the court of Mary, Queen of Scots.

Serves 10–12

275g plain flour
¼ tsp salt
¾ tsp baking powder
70g ground almonds
225g light muscovado sugar
Finely grated zest of 1 large
    unwaxed lemon

225g unsalted butter, softened
4 eggs, beaten
300g sultanas
200g currants
100g chopped mixed candied peel
1–2 tbsp whisky
About 18 blanched almonds

Grease and line a 20cm round deep cake tin (see page 11). Preheat the oven to 180°C.

Sift the flour with the salt, baking powder and ground almonds and set aside.

Put the sugar and lemon zest into a large mixing bowl or the bowl of a stand mixer and rub them together using your fingertips for a minute or so to release the fragrant oils. Add the butter and beat well until the mixture is very light and creamy.

Scrape down the sides of the bowl and gradually beat in the eggs, beating well after each addition and adding a tablespoon of the flour mixture with the last few additions of egg to prevent the mixture from splitting.

Mix a tablespoon of the flour mixture with the fruit and peel. Using a large metal spoon, lightly fold half of the remaining flour into the creamed mixture, then add the fruit/peel/flour mixture and gently combine. Finally, add the last of the flour mixture with a tablespoon of the whisky. Gently mix to a medium-soft consistency: the mixture should drop off the spoon when it is gently shaken. If it is a bit stiff, stir in another tablespoon of whisky.

Spoon the mixture into the prepared tin and spread it level using the back of a spoon, gently pressing the mixture down to make sure the fruit is covered by cake mixture. Dip your fingertips in water and press them over the surface to lightly moisten the top of the cake, which will help to prevent a dry crust forming before the cake has set. Tap the tin on the worktop to settle the mixture. Decorate the cake with neat circles of almonds.

Wrap a band of folded newspaper around the tin to help prevent the sides from over-baking and tie in place with string. Line a baking tray with several layers of newspaper and put the cake tin on top. Fill a roasting tin with water and put it near the bottom of the oven – the steamy atmosphere will help to keep the cake moist.

Bake the cake for 30 minutes. Reduce the oven temperature to 170°C and bake for a further 1½–1¾ hours or until a cocktail stick pushed into the centre of the cake comes out clean.

Put the tin on a wire rack and leave until cold before turning out. Wrap in foil and keep for a week to mature before cutting.

Rich Fruit Celebration Cake

A classic dark, rich fruit cake, loaded with dried fruits, candied peel, glacé cherries and chopped nuts, and finished with more than a splash of brandy, is always a winner for a celebration. Simply dusted with sugar and decorated with candles, or covered with marzipan and white icing, the cake is a special treat. It is worth making well ahead of time as the flavours will mature and improve over two to three months. The cake can be decorated just before it is needed.

Serves 12–16

150g blanched almonds	375g dark muscovado sugar
125g glacé morello cherries	6 eggs, beaten
375g plain flour	1 tbsp ground mixed spice
1kg dried mixed fruit or luxury	¼ tsp salt
dried fruit and peel mix	75g ground almonds
375g unsalted butter, softened	115ml brandy, plus 4 tbsp to finish

Grease and line a 23–24cm round deep cake tin (see page 11). Preheat the oven to 180°C.

Put the almonds into an ovenproof dish and toast in the oven until lightly coloured, about 7–8 minutes. Leave to cool, then chop roughly and set aside. Reduce the oven temperature to 150°C.

Halve the cherries, rinse with warm water to remove the sticky syrup and then pat dry. Put into a large bowl with 2 tablespoons of the flour, the dried fruit and the chopped almonds and toss gently to separate any clumps of fruit. Set aside.

Put the butter into the bowl of a stand mixer and beat with the paddle beater for a couple of minutes until creamy. Gradually beat in the sugar, then scrape down the sides of the bowl and beat thoroughly for about 5 minutes or until the mixture is lighter in colour and texture. Scrape down the sides of the bowl from time to time to make sure the ingredients are thoroughly combined.

Gradually beat in the eggs, beating well after each addition and adding a tablespoon of the flour with the last couple of additions to prevent the mixture from splitting.

Sift the remaining flour, mixed spice and salt into the bowl. Add the ground almonds and gently fold everything together using a large metal spoon. Add the fruit and nut mixture, along with any flour left in the base of the bowl, and the brandy. Carefully fold into the mixture, making sure the fruit is evenly distributed.

Spoon into the prepared tin and spread evenly. Tap the tin on the worktop to dislodge any air pockets, then make a slight hollow in the centre of the mixture to help the cake rise evenly and give a level surface that's easy to decorate.

Wrap a band of folded newspaper around the tin to help prevent the sides from over-baking and tie in place with string. Line a baking tray with several layers of newspaper and put the cake tin on top.

Bake for about 3–3½ hours or until golden brown and a cocktail stick pushed into the centre of the cake comes out clean. It is a good idea to rotate the cake a couple of times during baking so that it cooks evenly, and to check towards the end of the baking time that it is not getting too brown – if so, cover the top of the tin with greaseproof paper.

Put the tin on a wire rack and leave until cold before turning out.

Prick the top and the base of the cake several times with a cocktail stick or skewer, then put the cake on a plate and slowly trickle 4 tablespoons of brandy into the holes on both sides. Leave for about 20 minutes until the brandy has soaked in, then wrap in baking paper and foil and leave to mature for at least a month in a cool dry place.

Sponge Cakes

Elegant sponge cakes, feather-light and made from eggs, fine white sugar and carefully sifted white flour, arrived in royal palaces and grand houses along with Italian pastry cooks in the sixteenth century. Making them required skill and stamina, as the eggs and sugar had to be beaten in a copper bowl over warm water for 2 hours – to the 'ribbon' stage, as we still say – to make a thick, mousse-like foam. There were two ways to incorporate air: beating yolks and sugar and then folding in flour and a meringue made from the beaten whites, or beating whole eggs with sugar before working in flour. They were called 'biscuit cakes', as they were thinner and crisper and very different from yeasted fruit cakes.

The earliest recipe for a caraway seed cake, from the seventeenth century, mentions rubbing butter into finely sifted flour, then mixing in whipped egg whites, sweet wine, ale yeast and caraway comfits. Ground cloves and cinnamon were optional extras. This seems to be a kind of halfway house between traditions.

The French Revolution saw pastry cooks from aristocratic châteaux gaining employment in Britain's grandest establishments. They introduced more complex, sophisticated and, needless to say, expensive recipes. French-style cheesecakes and whipped cream cakes, along with cakes made from butter, cream, chocolate and vanilla, became fashionable among the wealthy towards the end of the eighteenth century and, as ever, fashions were imitated by the middle classes. In 1808 Jane Austen mentioned in a letter her fondness for sponge cakes.

The cakes were originally baked in wooden or metal hoops set on metal sheets, but delicate whisked sponges, with their crisp, fragile crusts, could be baked in shaped tin moulds to make a sculpted centrepiece for banquets. The flat-based round and square moulded metal cake tins we use today were developed in the mid-nineteenth century, after the invention of baking powder allowed sponges to be enriched with butter and still rise well while keeping a fine, light crumb. Ovens in private homes became more sophisticated as coal became cheaper. A gas cooker was displayed at the Great Exhibition in 1851, but these were slow to replace the coal-fired range and didn't become commonplace for another 60 or 70 years. Electric cookers appeared in the late 1920s but cooks found them hard to control because the power supply was inconsistent. As ever, cooks had to rely on their senses and judgement when cake baking.

Saffron, used for centuries to add a golden colour and honey scent to cakes, became briefly fashionable again after Queen Victoria's Golden Jubilee in 1887. The Queen emerged from mourning the death of Prince Albert to attend a banquet at Buckingham Palace served on gold plate, followed by many gold-themed balls, dinners, concerts and garden parties.

Sponge cakes are still subject to fashions: oversweet, multi-layered, multi-coloured confections have recently given way to flourless cakes, cakes made with very dark and bitter chocolate, and cakes finished with fresh fruits and berries.

Caraway Seed Cake

Caraway seeds have been eaten since Roman times to aid digestion, and they add a gentle aniseed flavour to cakes and bread. Caraway comfits – the seeds rolled in sugar – were enjoyed at court in Tudor times. Indeed, until the 1950s they could still be bought at some traditional confectioners and scattered over cakes before baking. Rich seed cakes were a staple of a fine Victorian tea table and this is one of the best recipes from that period. It gets better as it matures, so bake a day or so before cutting.

Serves 6–8

225g unsalted butter, softened	115g self-raising flour
225g caster sugar	¼ tsp salt
4 eggs, beaten	2 tsp caraway seeds
100g ground almonds	Icing sugar for dusting

Grease and base-line a 20cm springclip tin (see page 11). Preheat the oven to 180°C.

Put the butter into a mixing bowl or the bowl of a stand mixer and beat until very creamy. Gradually beat in the sugar, then scrape down the sides of the bowl and beat thoroughly for about 4 minutes or until the mixture is light in texture and colour.

Gradually beat in the eggs, beating well after each addition and scraping down the sides of the bowl from time to time to incorporate all the ingredients. Add a tablespoon of the ground almonds with each of the last two additions of egg to prevent the mixture from splitting.

Sift the remaining ground almonds, flour and salt into the bowl. Using a large metal spoon, carefully fold into the egg mixture until thoroughly combined, then gently fold in the caraway seeds. Transfer the mixture to the prepared tin and spread evenly.

Bake for about 50–55 minutes until golden brown and the top springs back when gently pressed in the centre.

Put the tin on a wire rack, run a round-bladed knife around the inside of the tin to loosen the cake, then carefully unclip and leave to cool. Dust with icing sugar.

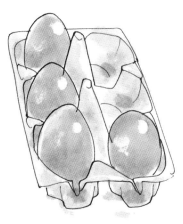

Espresso Swiss Roll

The classic Swiss roll is a whisked sponge made using just eggs, sugar and plain flour (plus a pinch of salt): there is no butter. It has a light, delicate crumb but is flexible enough to be rolled into a neat shape and sliced easily. For this version, finely ground espresso coffee is added to the flour, giving the sponge a speckled look. Liquid espresso coffee flavours the rich butter icing filling.

Serves 6–8

3 eggs
75g caster sugar, plus extra
   for dusting
75g plain flour
A good pinch of salt
1 tsp ground espresso coffee

For the filling
125g unsalted butter, at room
   temperature
250g icing sugar
3 tbsp strong espresso coffee,
   at room temperature

Grease and line a Swiss roll tin about 20 x 30cm (see page 11). Preheat the oven to 220°C.

Break the eggs into a large mixing bowl or the bowl of a stand mixer and whisk on high speed for a few seconds until slightly frothy. Add the sugar and whisk on high speed for 4–5 minutes until the mixture is very thick, pale and mousse-like and falls in a ribbon-like trail when the whisk is lifted out of the mixture.

Sift the flour, salt and ground coffee onto a sheet of greaseproof paper, then sift about half of it a second time directly onto the mousse. Using a large metal spoon, gently fold in the flour mixture. Sift the remaining flour mixture into the bowl and gently fold in until you can no longer see any streaks of flour. Gently scrape down the sides of the bowl and check the bottom of the bowl for any uncombined mixture.

Gently pour the sponge mixture into the prepared tin and spread it evenly, taking care with the corners. Bake for about 9–10 minutes until the sponge is golden, starting to shrink from the sides of the tin, and is springy to the touch.

While the sponge is baking, lay a sheet of baking paper (about 30 x 40cm) on the worktop and sprinkle lightly with caster sugar. As soon as the sponge is ready, flip the tin over, onto the baking paper. Carefully lift off the tin and the lining paper.

Using a large sharp knife make a shallow cut across one short end of the sponge, about 2cm in from the edge – this will help to give the roll a neat spiral when it is sliced. Starting from the end with the cut, gently roll up the hot sponge with the paper so that the paper is rolled inside. Place the roll on a wire rack to cool completely.

Meanwhile, make the filling: beat the butter until creamy. Sift the icing sugar into the bowl and add the coffee. Starting slowly, and gradually increasing the speed, beat everything together until smooth and thick.

To finish the cake, carefully unroll the sponge and trim off the firm edges with a sharp knife. Spread with the filling and then gently re-roll. Put the roll on a serving plate and sprinkle with a little more caster sugar.

Spiced Carrot Cake

During the Second World War, when sugar was rationed, the Ministry of Food encouraged people to grow carrots for use in puddings and cakes, but it was the more extravagant carrot cakes of the 1970s, flavoured with spices, nuts and sometimes raisins and grated coconut, and finished with a rich cream-cheese filling and topping, that became the classic we love today.

Serves 10–12

75g pecan halves
225g self-raising flour
1 tsp baking powder
¼ tsp salt
2 tsp ground cinnamon
1½ tsp ground ginger
¼ tsp grated nutmeg
225g light muscovado sugar
4 eggs, beaten
225ml light or mild olive oil or
  sunflower oil
200g grated carrots
40g drained stem ginger, grated or
  finely chopped

For the filling and topping
200g mascarpone cheese, well
  chilled
50g icing sugar
50g unsalted butter, softened
Finely grated zest of 1 unwaxed
  lemon
1 tbsp lemon juice, or to taste
1 tbsp ginger syrup from the jar
Pecan halves to decorate

Grease and base-line two 20cm round deep sandwich tins (see page 11). Preheat the oven to 180°C.

Put the pecans into an ovenproof dish and toast in the oven until lightly coloured, about 5–7 minutes. Leave to cool, then chop fairly coarsely. Set aside.

Sift the flour, baking powder, salt, cinnamon, ground ginger and grated nutmeg into a large mixing bowl. Stir in the sugar. Combine the eggs with the oil and add to the bowl along with the grated carrots, stem ginger and chopped nuts. Mix thoroughly with a wooden spoon, then divide between the two prepared tins and spread evenly.

Bake for 25–30 minutes until firm to the touch and a cocktail stick pushed into the centre of each cake comes out clean. Put the tins on a wire rack, run a round-bladed knife around the inside of the tins to loosen the cakes, leave to firm up for 5 minutes, then turn out and leave to cool.

To make the filling and topping: put the mascarpone into a mixing bowl and stir until smooth, then sift the icing sugar into the bowl, add the butter, lemon zest and juice and the ginger syrup and mix thoroughly.

Put one sponge, crust side down, on a serving plate and spread with half of the filling mixture. Top with the second sponge, crust side uppermost, and spread with the remaining mixture. Decorate with pecans. Keep cool or in the fridge until ready to serve.

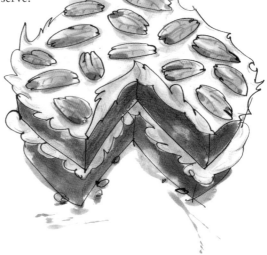

Coffee and Walnut Cake

An irresistible combination of a light, well-flavoured sponge with a buttery topping and a filling rich with coffee and nuts makes this cake one of the all-time favourites. The recipe first appeared in print in a 1934 advert for McDougalls' self-raising flour. The flavours develop as it matures, so plan on making a day or so ahead.

Serves 6–8

100g walnut pieces
175g unsalted butter, softened
145g golden caster sugar
1 tbsp golden syrup
3 eggs, beaten
175g self-raising flour
1 tbsp instant coffee, dissolved in
   1 tbsp boiling water and left
   to cool
A good pinch of salt

For the filling and topping
125g unsalted butter
300g icing sugar
3 tbsp instant coffee dissolved in
   2 tbsp boiling water
4 tbsp whipping, single or double
   cream
Walnut halves to decorate

Grease and base-line two 20cm round deep sandwich tins (see page 11). Preheat the oven to 180°C.

Put the walnut pieces into an ovenproof dish and toast in the oven until lightly coloured and fragrant, about 8 minutes. Leave to cool, then chop fairly coarsely. Set aside 40g of the nuts for the filling.

Put the butter into a mixing bowl and beat until creamy, with the consistency of mayonnaise, then beat in the sugar and golden syrup. Scrape down the sides of the bowl and then beat thoroughly for about 4 minutes until light and fluffy. Scrape down the sides of the bowl again and gradually beat in the eggs, beating well after each addition and adding a tablespoon of the flour with each of the last two additions to prevent the mixture from splitting.

Add the 60g of chopped walnuts and the cool coffee. Sift the remaining flour and salt on top and gently fold everything together using a large metal spoon until thoroughly combined. Divide the mixture between the two prepared tins and spread evenly.

Bake for 20–25 minutes until the sponges are golden brown and spring back when gently pressed in the centre.

Carefully turn out onto a wire rack and leave to cool.

Meanwhile, make the filling and topping: gently heat the butter in a small pan until melted, then bring to the boil and let it bubble away until the solids at the bottom turn a rich gold colour. Meanwhile, sift the icing sugar into a mixing bowl. Add the hot butter, coffee and cream to the bowl and beat well to make a smooth, thick icing. Stir in the reserved chopped nuts, then set aside until firm enough to spread easily.

Put one sponge, crust side down, on a serving plate and spread with half the coffee and nut mixture. Top with the second sponge, crust side uppermost, and spread with the remaining mixture. Decorate with walnut halves and leave to firm up.

Chocolate Pecan Fudge Cake (GF)

This is a very rich, intense chocolate cake flavoured with a dash of strong black coffee or dark rum, with nuts for texture. You will need an electric whisk or mixer: the eggs (whisked with sugar to triple their volume) provide the structure to hold the mixture together during baking as it is made without flour.

Serves 6–8

100g pecan halves
275g dark chocolate (about
    70 per cent cocoa solids)
145g unsalted butter, at room
    temperature, diced
1 tbsp strong espresso-type coffee
    or dark rum

40g cocoa powder
4 eggs
A good pinch of salt
200g golden caster sugar
Icing sugar for dusting

Grease and base-line a 20cm square cake tin (see page 11). Preheat the oven to 180°C.

Set aside 20g of the best-looking pecans for the topping, then put the rest into an ovenproof dish and lightly toast in the oven, about 5–8 minutes. Leave to cool, then chop fairly coarsely. Set aside.

Chop the chocolate into evenly sized pieces and put into a heatproof bowl with the butter and coffee or rum. Set the bowl over a pan of steaming hot but not boiling water; don't let the base of the bowl touch the water. Leave to melt; avoid stirring – just tilt the bowl from time to time and gently press any unmelted chocolate under the surface. Remove the bowl from the pan, gently stir the melted mixture, then sift the cocoa powder into the bowl and carefully mix in. Leave to cool.

Break the eggs into a large mixing bowl or the bowl of a stand mixer, add the salt and whisk on high speed for a few seconds until frothy. Whisk in the sugar and continue whisking until the mixture is very light and has tripled in volume – about 4–5 minutes.

Using a large metal spoon, carefully fold in the chocolate mixture, followed by the chopped pecans. Gently transfer the mixture to the prepared tin and then scatter over the reserved pecan halves.

Bake for about 30 minutes until just firm to the touch – the centre will still be moist if tested with a cocktail stick (avoid overcooking as this will make the cake more difficult to cut neatly).

Put the tin on a wire rack and leave to cool completely before turning out. Wrap in foil and keep overnight before dusting with icing sugar and cutting.

Victoria Sandwich Cake

The classic jam-and-cream sponge cake is named after Queen Victoria, who was fond of afternoon tea and cake. Thanks to the invention of baking powder in 1843, Victorian bakers were able to add butter to their sponge cakes, resulting in a richer, firmer sponge that was ideal for sandwiching with filling. Baking powder is a chemical raising agent, a combination of bicarbonate of soda (an alkali) and cream of tartar (a mild acid), which releases small bubbles of carbon dioxide in the moist mixture, pushing it up in the heat of the oven before the cake sets. This recipe uses self-raising flour, with its inclusion of chemical raising agents in the exact ratio needed for cakes, which is very handy.

Serves 6–8

175g unsalted butter, softened
175g caster sugar
3 eggs
½ tsp vanilla extract
175g self-raising flour
¼ tsp salt
1 tbsp boiling water

For the filling
175g good raspberry or strawberry conserve or jam
175ml double or whipping cream, well chilled
½ tsp vanilla extract
1 tbsp caster sugar
Icing sugar for dusting

Grease and base-line two 20cm round deep sandwich tins (see page 11). Preheat the oven to 180°C.

Put the butter into a mixing bowl and beat for a minute or so until very creamy. Beat in the sugar, then scrape down the sides of the bowl and beat thoroughly until very light in colour and texture, scraping down the sides of the bowl from time to time to incorporate all the mixture.

In another bowl, break up the eggs with a fork and mix in the vanilla until combined. Gradually beat the eggs into the butter mixture, beating well after each addition and adding a tablespoon of the flour with each of the last two additions to prevent the mixture from splitting.

Sift the remaining flour and salt into the bowl and carefully fold in using a large metal spoon. Finally, fold in the boiling water. Divide the mixture between the two prepared tins and spread evenly.

Bake for about 20–25 minutes until the sponges are a light golden brown and spring back when gently pressed in the centre.

Run a round-bladed knife around the inside of each tin to loosen the sponges, then carefully turn out onto a wire rack and leave to cool completely.

Put one sponge, crust side down, on a serving plate and spread it with a thick layer of conserve or jam, right up to the edges. Whip the cream until it stands in soft peaks, add the vanilla and sugar and whip briefly until slightly thicker. Spoon on top of the jam and spread almost to the edges of the sponge. Gently put the second sponge on top, golden crust side uppermost. Dust with icing sugar. Keep cool until ready to slice.

Parkin

This dark, sticky, glossy-topped cake is a favourite from Yorkshire and Lancashire, a robust version of gingerbread that includes oatmeal. It is made using the melting method, all in one pan. There is no standard recipe as it was originally made with what was locally available: butter is now usual but lard or dripping were once fairly commonplace; the sugar can be light or dark muscovado, caster, granulated or demerara; and the liquid can be milk, water, stout or, as here, a fiery non-alcoholic ginger beer. Fancier recipes add chopped candied peel or almonds. Enjoy parkin at its sticky best several days after baking, with a wedge of Lancashire cheese.

Serves 8–9

100g unsalted butter, diced	1 egg, at room temperature
100g dark muscovado sugar	230g plain flour
175g golden syrup	¼ tsp salt
175g black treacle	1 tbsp ground ginger
230g medium oatmeal	2 tsp ground mixed spice
125ml fiery ginger beer	1 tbsp baking powder

Grease and base-line a 20cm square deep cake tin (see page 11). Preheat the oven to 180°C.

Weigh the butter, sugar, syrup and treacle into a pan large enough to hold all the ingredients. Melt gently over a medium-low heat, stirring with a wooden spoon until the mixture is smooth.

Remove the pan from the heat and stir in the oatmeal. Combine the ginger beer and the egg, then stir into the pan.

Finally, sift the flour, salt, ginger, mixed spice and baking powder into the pan and mix thoroughly to make a thick, batter-like mixture.

Pour and scrape the sticky mixture into the prepared tin and bake for about 45–50 minutes until just firm when gently pressed in the centre.

Put the tin on a wire rack and run a round-bladed knife around the inside of the tin to loosen the cake – don't worry if the cake starts to shrink. Leave until completely cold and then remove from the tin. Wrap in foil and, ideally, keep for at least 5 days before cutting.

Mocha Cake

The term 'mocha' now means a combination of coffee and chocolate, either as a drink or as flavours in cooking; originally it meant the finest Arabica coffee beans that came from the port of Mokha in Yemen. Dark chocolate and coffee make an excellent pairing. This creamed espresso sponge, speckled with grated dark chocolate and sandwiched with a mocha butter icing, improves over a day or two as the flavours mature.

Serves 6–8

2 tbsp double espresso (or 1½ tbsp instant coffee dissolved in 2 tbsp boiling water)
175g unsalted butter, softened
175g golden caster sugar
3 eggs, beaten
175g self-raising flour
¼ tsp salt
50g dark chocolate (about 75–80 per cent cocoa solids), grated or finely chopped

For the filling
50g dark chocolate (about 75–80 per cent cocoa solids), roughly chopped
1 tbsp double espresso (or 1 tbsp instant coffee dissolved in 1 tbsp boiling water)
60g unsalted butter, softened
2 tbsp golden syrup

To finish
Icing sugar for dusting
Chocolate coffee beans (optional)

Grease and base-line two 20cm round deep sandwich tins (see page 11). Preheat the oven to 180°C.

Make the espresso or instant coffee and leave to cool.

Put the butter into a mixing bowl and beat for a minute or so until very creamy, then gradually beat in the sugar. Scrape down the sides of the bowl and beat for another 3–4 minutes until the mixture is light and fluffy.

Scrape down the sides of the bowl again and gradually beat in the eggs, beating well after each addition and adding a tablespoon of the flour with each of the last two additions to prevent the mixture from splitting.

Sift the remaining flour and the salt into the bowl and gently fold into the mixture using a large metal spoon. Add the cooled coffee and grated chocolate and mix until thoroughly combined. Divide the mixture between the prepared tins and spread evenly.

Bake for about 20–25 minutes or until the sponges spring back when gently pressed in the centre. Run a round-bladed knife around the inside of each tin to loosen the cakes, then carefully turn out onto a wire rack and leave to cool.

Meanwhile, make the filling: put the chocolate and just-warm coffee into a heatproof bowl. Set over a pan of steaming hot but not boiling water and leave to melt; don't let the base of the bowl touch the water. Remove the bowl from the heat, stir gently once or twice until just combined, then add the butter and golden syrup. Stir gently until smooth, then leave to cool and firm up, stirring now and then until the filling is firm enough to spread easily.

Put one sponge, crust side down, on a serving plate and spread with the filling. Top with the second sponge, crust side uppermost, and press it gently in place. Dust with icing sugar and scatter over the chocolate coffee beans, if using.

Blood Orange Poppyseed Cake

This is a feather-light whisked sponge, flecked with tiny dark grey poppyseeds and infused with fresh orange: add a dramatic flash of red when blood oranges are in season, but any large, ripe, well-flavoured oranges work well. Check that your poppyseeds are really fresh, as they rapidly lose their nutty, slightly sweet flavour if kept too long: if they taste slightly bitter or smell musty then please don't use. This is a good cake when something not-too-rich or sweet is required.

Serves 8–9

75g unsalted butter, diced
125g golden caster sugar
Finely grated zest of 1 large
    unwaxed blood orange
4 eggs
125g plain flour

A good pinch of salt
10g poppyseeds

For the syrup
Finely grated zest and juice of
    1 large unwaxed blood orange
50g golden caster sugar

Grease and base-line a 20cm square cake tin (see page 11). Preheat the oven to 180°C.

Melt the butter in a small pan over a low heat, then set aside to cool.

Put the sugar and orange zest into a large mixing bowl and rub them together using your fingertips for a minute or so to release the fragrant oils. Add the eggs and whisk with an electric mixer for about 5 minutes until the mixture is very thick and mousse-like and falls in a ribbon-like trail when the whisk is lifted out of the mixture.

Sift the flour and salt into the bowl and gently fold in using a large metal spoon. When you can no longer see any streaks of flour, trickle in the melted butter around the sides of the bowl. Sprinkle the poppyseeds on top and carefully fold in. Transfer the mixture to the prepared tin and spread evenly.

Bake for about 30 minutes until the sponge is golden, has started to shrink from the sides of the tin and springs back when gently pressed.

Carefully turn out onto a wire rack and leave to cool.

Meanwhile, make the syrup: put the orange zest, 75ml of the squeezed juice and the sugar into a small pan and heat gently, stirring until the sugar has dissolved. Bring to the boil and simmer for a minute or two to make a light syrup.

Put the sponge on a serving plate and spoon over the hot syrup. Leave to stand for about 30 minutes for the sponge to absorb the syrup before cutting.

Lemon Cream Roll (GF)

Ground almonds give this flourless whisked sponge a light and moist texture. The rich, well-flavoured lemon mousse filling is very easy: a cheat's version of lemon curd combined with whipped cream.

Serves 6–8

125g golden caster sugar
2 medium–large unwaxed lemons
4 eggs
A good pinch of salt
100g ground almonds

For the filling
75g unsalted butter
Finely grated zest and juice of
   1 medium–large unwaxed lemon

125g icing sugar
2 tsp limoncello (optional)
150ml double or whipping cream,
   well chilled

To finish
Caster sugar for dusting
Lemon zest, cut into fine shreds

Grease and line a Swiss roll tin about 20 x 30cm (see page 11). Preheat the oven to 180°C.

Weigh 120g of the sugar into a mixing bowl. Grate the lemon zest onto the sugar and then rub together using your fingertips to release the fragrant oils. Halve the lemons and squeeze the juice; set aside.

Separate the eggs, putting the whites and the salt into a spotlessly clean large mixing bowl and adding the yolks to the lemon sugar.

Using an electric mixer, whisk the egg whites until they form soft peaks. Whisk in the reserved sugar on high speed for a few seconds until the mixture is stiff and glossy; set aside.

Using the same whisk (no need to wash it), whisk the egg yolks and lemon sugar for 3–4 minutes until very thick and mousse-like. Using a large metal spoon, gently fold in the ground almonds and lemon juice.

Fold the egg whites into the mixture in three batches. Transfer the mixture to the prepared tin and spread evenly, making sure the corners are well filled.

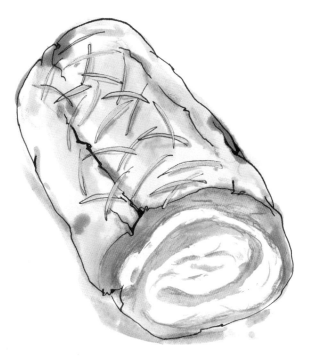

Bake for about 20 minutes until the top is golden and the sponge feels just firm but springy. Put the tin on a wire rack, then cover the top lightly with a sheet of greaseproof paper and then a damp tea towel (try not to let them touch the surface of the sponge): this will make it easier to roll up the sponge later on. Leave to cool completely.

Meanwhile, make the filling: put the butter, lemon zest and juice into a small pan. Heat gently until the butter has melted, then turn up the heat and stir until the mixture boils. Remove the pan from the heat.

Quickly sift the icing sugar into a heatproof bowl and then pour the hot butter mixture onto the sugar; beat well with a wooden spoon until smooth. Mix in the limoncello, if using. Leave to cool, then chill, stirring frequently, until the mixture has the consistency of mayonnaise. Whip the chilled cream until it forms very soft peaks, then gently fold in the lemon mixture.

Dust a large sheet of greaseproof paper with caster sugar. Turn out the sponge onto the paper and carefully lift off the tin and the lining paper. Trim off any ragged edges with a sharp knife, then make a shallow cut across one short end of the sponge, about 2cm in from the edge. Spread the lemon mixture almost to the edges of the sponge, then gently roll up, from the end with the cut, using the greaseproof paper to help you shape the roll.

When you finish the roll, wrap the paper tightly around it. The sponge will crack – maybe a little, maybe a lot – but the paper will help to hold it together. Cover and chill for at least 2 hours to firm up.

Remove the paper and transfer the cake to a serving plate. Dust with more caster sugar and finish with shreds of lemon zest.

Flourless Chocolate Cream Cake (GF)

A light-textured but utterly luxurious mousse-like cake made with mascarpone. This thick, rich, soft Italian cheese is made from fresh cream and has a slightly sweet taste, which works well with dark chocolate. Use gluten-free or original digestive biscuits for the chocolate base.

Serves 6–8

For the base
200g digestive biscuits (gluten-free or original)
50g unsalted butter, diced
50g dark chocolate (about 70 per cent cocoa solids), finely chopped

For the cake
2 eggs
A good pinch of salt
75g caster sugar

150ml double cream, well chilled
225g mascarpone cheese
50g dark chocolate (about 70 per cent cocoa solids), very finely chopped
4 tbsp cocoa powder, sifted
45g ground almonds
1–2 tbsp double espresso coffee, cooled, to taste (you could also use brandy, rum or amaretto)
Icing sugar for dusting

Thoroughly grease a 20cm springclip tin (see page 11).

To make the base: crush the biscuits to a fine powder and tip into a mixing bowl. Put the butter and chopped chocolate into a heatproof bowl and gently melt over a pan of steaming hot but not boiling water; don't let the base of the bowl touch the water. Remove from the heat, stir gently until smooth, then stir into the biscuit crumbs. When thoroughly combined tip the mixture into the prepared tin and press over the base, using the back of a spoon, to make an even layer. Chill while you make the cake mixture.

Preheat the oven to 170°C.

Separate the eggs, putting the whites and the salt into a spotlessly clean large mixing bowl and the yolks into another mixing bowl. Using an electric mixer, whisk the whites until they form soft peaks and then whisk in a tablespoon of the sugar, whisking for a minute or so until stiff peaks form. Set aside.

Using the same whisk (no need to wash it), whisk the egg yolks and the remaining sugar until very thick and mousse-like. In another bowl (again, no need to wash the whisk), whip the cream until it forms very soft peaks and then gently stir in the mascarpone.

Stir the cream and mascarpone mixture into the egg yolks, then gently stir in the chopped chocolate, cocoa powder, ground almonds and cold coffee. Using a large metal spoon, fold the egg whites into the mixture in three batches.

Spoon the mixture over the chilled base, then bake for about 60–70 minutes or until just set when the tin is gently jiggled.

Put the tin on a wire rack and run a round-bladed knife around the inside of the tin to loosen the cake. Leave to cool and firm up for about 20 minutes before unclipping – the cake will shrink as it cools.

Dust with icing sugar just before cutting.

Clotted Cream Strawberry Sponge

Clotted cream is a speciality of Cornwall and Devon, in England's South West, and along with fresh scones and jam is one of the essentials of a cream tea. Historians suggest that the recipe for turning milk into a very rich and thick cream, with a high fat content of around 60 per cent and spreadable like butter, dates back 2,000 years, when Phoenician traders brought their recipes as well as goods in exchange for Cornish tin from local mines. The cream makes a light, moist sponge base for perfectly ripe and juicy strawberries soaked in an orange syrup. This cake is ideal for a summer afternoon tea party.

Serves 10–12

---

3 eggs
225g caster sugar
½ vanilla pod
225g clotted cream
220g self-raising flour
A good pinch of salt
1 large unwaxed orange

For the topping
450g ripe strawberries, hulled
2 tbsp caster sugar
⅛–¼ tsp ground black pepper,
   to taste
Clotted cream to serve

Grease and base-line a 23cm springclip tin (see page 11). Preheat the oven to 180°C.

Break the eggs into a large mixing bowl or the bowl of a stand mixer, whisk with an electric mixer for a few seconds until frothy and then whisk in the sugar. With the tip of a small sharp knife, split open the vanilla pod and scrape out the seeds into the bowl (keep the pod for making custard or ice cream another day).

Whisk on high speed for about 4 minutes until the mixture is very thick and mousse-like and falls in a distinct ribbon-like trail when the whisk is lifted out of the mixture.

Give the cream a stir in its tub, then spoon into the mixing bowl and gently stir in. Sift the flour and salt onto the mixture and carefully fold in using a large metal spoon.

Finely grate the zest from the orange and set aside for the topping. Halve and squeeze out the juice. Add 1 tablespoon of juice to the sponge mixture and fold in. Set aside the remaining juice for the topping.

Transfer the sponge mixture to the prepared tin and spread evenly.

Bake for about 40 minutes or until golden and firm to the touch and a cocktail stick pushed into the centre comes out clean.

Put the tin on a wire rack, run a round-bladed knife around the inside of the tin to loosen the cake – it will shrink a little – then leave to firm up for 5 minutes before turning out. Leave to cool completely.

To make the topping: halve or quarter the strawberries, depending on size. Put in a bowl, add the reserved grated orange zest and 4 tablespoons of the juice, the sugar and a little black pepper to taste – enough to add a little kick. Mix well, then cover and chill.

Just before serving, put the cake on a serving plate. Stir the strawberry mixture and then spoon the berries and juice over the sponge. Serve in thick wedges with clotted cream.

Fresh Orange Surprise Cake

The crisp, bitter chocolate covering disguises a fine whisked sponge with intense flavour. After baking, the sponge is drenched in orange syrup and then coated in chocolate. In Edwardian times a light fruit cake or delicate sponge like this would be offered at the end of a 'ladies' luncheon'.

Serves 6–8

120g unsalted butter
150g plain flour
1 tsp baking powder
A good pinch of salt
50g ground almonds
200g caster sugar
Finely grated zest and juice of
   2 oranges
3 eggs

For the soaking syrup
100ml freshly squeezed orange
   juice (about 2 oranges)
80g caster sugar
1–2 tbsp orange liqueur (optional)

For the chocolate icing
150g dark chocolate (about
    70 per cent cocoa solids)
50g unsalted butter, softened

Grease and base-line a 20cm springclip tin (see page 11). Preheat the oven to 180°C.

Melt the butter in a small pan over a low heat and then set aside to cool. Sift the flour, baking powder, salt and ground almonds into a bowl, or onto a sheet of greaseproof paper, and set aside. Set aside 2 tablespoons of the sugar.

Tip the remaining sugar into a large mixing bowl, add the orange zest and rub them together using your fingertips to release the fragrant oils.

Measure 100ml of the squeezed juice and set aside.

Separate the eggs, putting the whites into a spotlessly clean large mixing bowl, and adding the yolks to the orange sugar. Whisk the egg whites until they form soft peaks, then whisk in the reserved sugar on high speed for a few seconds to form stiff peaks. Set aside.

Using the same whisk, combine the yolks and sugar until very thick and mousse-like. Whisk in the reserved 100ml orange juice – the mixture will deflate. Sift the flour and almond mixture a second time directly into the bowl and gently fold in using a large metal spoon. Fold in the cooled melted butter, followed by the beaten egg whites in three batches.

Gently pour the mixture into the prepared tin and bake for about 35–40 minutes until golden and just firm when pressed and a cocktail stick pushed into the centre comes out clean.

While the cake is baking, make the soaking syrup: put the orange juice and sugar into a small pan and heat gently, stirring until the sugar has dissolved, then bring to the boil and remove from the heat. Stir in the liqueur, if using.

Put the cake in its tin on a wire rack, prick the sponge all over with a cocktail stick or skewer and then slowly spoon the warm syrup over the cake until it is all absorbed. Leave to cool before removing from the tin.

When ready to ice, chop the chocolate into evenly sized pieces and gently melt in a heatproof bowl set over a pan of steaming hot but not boiling water; don't let the base of the bowl touch the water. Remove the bowl from the heat, add the butter and gently stir until melted and smooth (don't overwork the mixture or it will seize up). Leave to cool until thickened but still fluid.

Put the sponge on a wire rack set over a plate to catch the drips. Pour the chocolate icing over the cake, easing it down the sides to cover neatly, and leave to set.

Transfer to a serving plate. Use a warmed sharp knife to cut neat slices.

Chocolate Celebration Cake

A gorgeous special occasion cake made from three layers of rich chocolate sponge – made the quick all-in-one way with the addition of chocolate chips – sandwiched with milk chocolate fudge and then covered in darker chocolate frosting. You can leave the cake plain and unadorned, cover it in chocolate curls or sprinkles, or add piped decorations and candles. It is best made a day or so before cutting.

Serves 10–12

200g self-raising flour
75g cocoa powder
¼ tsp salt
1 tsp baking powder
250g golden caster sugar
250g unsalted butter, softened
6 eggs
1 tsp vanilla extract
1 tbsp milk
90g chocolate chips (dark, milk or
    white chocolate)

For the fudge filling
80g milk chocolate (with around
    40 per cent cocoa solids)

80g unsalted butter, softened
75g icing sugar
1½ tbsp cocoa powder

For the chocolate frosting
100g dark chocolate (about
    70 per cent cocoa solids)
100g unsalted butter, softened
100g icing sugar
2 tbsp cocoa powder

To finish
Grated chocolate, chocolate curls
    or sprinkles to cover the sides
    (optional)

Grease and base-line three 20cm round deep sandwich tins (see page 11). Preheat the oven to 180°C.

Sift the flour, cocoa powder, salt and baking powder into a large mixing bowl or the bowl of a stand mixer fitted with the paddle beater. Add the sugar and the butter to the bowl. Beat the eggs with the vanilla and milk and pour in. Starting slowly, beat with a wooden spoon or the mixer, gradually increasing the speed as the ingredients start to come together. Scrape down the sides of the bowl from time to time to incorporate all the ingredients and continue beating until the mixture is silky smooth and light. Stir in the chocolate chips.

Divide the mixture equally between the three prepared tins and spread evenly (if necessary, bake in batches, wiping out and preparing the tins as before).

Bake for about 15 minutes until the sponges are well risen, starting to shrink from the sides of the tins and feel just firm when gently pressed in the centre.

Put the tins on a wire rack, run a round-bladed knife around the inside of each tin to loosen the sponges and carefully turn out onto the rack to cool.

Meanwhile, make the fudge filling: chop the chocolate into evenly sized pieces and put into a heatproof bowl large enough to hold all the ingredients. Set over a pan of steaming hot but not boiling water; don't let the base of the bowl touch the water. Leave to melt gently, then remove the bowl from the heat, add the butter in small pieces and gently stir in. When melted and smooth sift the icing sugar and cocoa into the bowl and mix with a wooden spoon to make a smooth, thick, spreadable filling.

To assemble the cake: put one sponge, crust side down, on a serving plate or cake board. Spread with half the fudge filling and then top with a second sponge, crust side uppermost. Spread with the remaining filling and then put the third sponge on top, crust side uppermost.

Make the chocolate frosting in the same way as the filling: gently melt the dark chocolate, then stir in the butter followed by the sifted icing sugar and cocoa. Using an off-set palette knife, spread the frosting over the top and sides of the cake, to completely cover it.

If you like, press grated chocolate, curls or sprinkles around the sides of the cake while the frosting is still soft. Leave the top to firm up before adding a piped decoration or centrepiece.

Store in an airtight container at cool room temperature for a day or so before cutting.

Brown Butter Pound Cake

A classic pound cake is made with equal weights of butter, sugar, eggs and flour and needs plenty of beating to add air and lightness, but the flavour has always been a testament to the fine ingredients. Here, the butter is gently cooked to add a nuttiness to the sponge, and toasted nuts are folded in, though you could replace them with crystallised fruits or chocolate chips. It is baked in a Bundt tin – a shaped or fluted deep ring mould – making it an elegant cake for a tea party.

The Bundt tin was designed in 1950 by the owner of Nordic Ware, a kitchenware company in Minnesota, USA. The aluminium tin with its centre cone made it easy to bake large or dense mixtures evenly – in particular the German-style kugelhopf (traditionally baked in a ridged ceramic ring mould), which the Minneapolis chapter of the Hadassah organisation of Jewish women wished to recreate. In 1966 the Bundt tin was used to bake the 'Tunnel of Fudge Cake', winner of a national baking competition, and the tin became a kitchen icon.

Serves 10–12

230g unsalted butter
100g pecans or blanched hazelnuts
  (or 70g chopped crystallised
  fruits or chocolate chips)
230g caster sugar
4 eggs

3 tbsp milk, brandy or bourbon
230g self-raising flour
¼ tsp salt
¼ tsp grated nutmeg
¼ tsp ground mace
Icing sugar for dusting

Thoroughly grease a 23cm diameter Bundt tin.

Melt the butter in a small pan over a medium-low heat, then let it bubble away, stirring frequently, until the solids at the bottom are a light golden brown: this will take 3–4 minutes. Pour the contents of the pan into a heatproof bowl and chill, stirring now and then, until the butter has the consistency of mayonnaise.

Meanwhile, preheat the oven to 180°C.

Put the nuts, if using, into an ovenproof dish and toast in the oven until lightly coloured and fragrant, about 5–8 minutes. Leave to cool, then roughly chop and set aside.

Put the creamy chilled butter and the sugar into a mixing bowl and beat thoroughly with an electric mixer. Scrape down the sides of the bowl, then beat the eggs with the milk, brandy or bourbon in a jug. Gradually beat into the butter mixture, beating well after each addition and adding a tablespoon of the flour with each of the last two additions to prevent the mixture from splitting.

Remove a tablespoon of the remaining flour and set aside. Sift the rest of the flour, salt, nutmeg and mace into the bowl and gently fold in using a large metal spoon. Mix the reserved tablespoon of flour with the chopped nuts, or the crystallised fruits or chocolate chips, and add to the bowl. Carefully mix until evenly distributed, then transfer to the prepared tin and spread evenly. Tap the tin on the worktop to settle the mixture, then bake for 50–60 minutes or until a cocktail stick pushed into the cake halfway between the centre funnel and the sides comes out clean.

Put the tin on a wire rack and leave to firm up for about 10 minutes, then carefully turn out and leave to cool.

Dust with icing sugar before cutting into thick wedges.

Two-Chocolate Ripple Cake

This impressively shaped, decorated cake uses two types of chocolate – dark chocolate (with about 70 per cent cocoa solids) and a top-quality white chocolate (with about 30 per cent cocoa solids) – along with cocoa powder. Add vivid chopped pistachios to the chocolate icings or, for a party, fill the centre with chocolate truffles or mini eggs.

Serves 10–12

250g unsalted butter, softened
250g caster sugar
5 eggs, beaten
250g self-raising flour
¼ tsp salt
75g dark chocolate (about 70 per cent cocoa solids), chopped
75g white chocolate (about 30 per cent cocoa solids), chopped
1 tbsp cocoa powder
1 tsp vanilla extract

To decorate
50g dark chocolate (about 70 per cent cocoa solids), chopped
50g white chocolate (about 30 per cent cocoa solids), chopped
100g unsalted butter, softened
Chopped pistachios, chocolate truffles or mini eggs (optional)

Thoroughly grease a 23cm diameter Bundt tin. Preheat the oven to 180°C.

Put the butter into a large mixing bowl and beat until creamy, then beat in the sugar. Scrape down the sides of the bowl and beat well for several minutes until the mixture is light and fluffy.

Gradually beat in the eggs, beating well after each addition and adding a tablespoon of the flour with each of the last few additions to prevent the mixture from splitting.

Sift the remaining flour and the salt into the bowl and gently fold in using a large metal spoon. Spoon half of the mixture into another bowl.

Put the chopped dark chocolate into a heatproof bowl set over a pan of steaming hot but not boiling water and gently melt; don't let the base of the bowl touch the water. Remove from the pan, stir gently just until smooth and then leave to cool. Melt the white chocolate in the same way, taking great care not to overheat it as it melts at a lower temperature.

Sift the cocoa powder into one portion of the sponge mixture, add the cooled melted dark chocolate and gently mix together.

Add the vanilla extract and cooled melted white chocolate to the second portion of the sponge mixture and gently mix together.

Spoon the mixtures alternately into the prepared tin, then slowly swirl a small knife through the mixtures to create the marbling.

Bake for about 50 minutes or until a cocktail stick inserted into the thickest part of the cake comes out clean.

Put the tin on a wire rack and gently run a round-bladed knife around the top inside edge of the tin and around the centre funnel to loosen the cake, then leave for about 15 minutes for the crust to firm up before carefully turning out. Leave to cool completely.

Meanwhile, make the chocolate icings: melt each chocolate in a separate bowl as before. Remove from the heat, then add 50g of butter to each bowl and gently stir until smooth and glossy. Leave to cool until thickened but still fluid and then spoon over the cooled cake, allowing the chocolate to flow down the sides. If using chopped nuts, add them before the chocolate sets, otherwise leave until firm before filling the centre with chocolate truffles or mini eggs, if using.

Sachertorte

A Viennese icon, said to have been invented in 1832 by a 16-year-old apprentice, Franz Sacher, who stepped in when Chambellier, chef to Prince Metternich, the Chancellor of the Austrian Empire, fell ill. The exact recipe for the dense, chocolate-rich sponge with a thick apricot jam layer and glossy chocolate covering remains under lock and key at the Hotel Sacher in Vienna, though Demel's pastry shop makes a similar version, 'Eduard Sacher Torte', named after Franz's son. There is much dispute about whether the sponge should be split and sandwiched with more jam, or whether rum should be sprinkled over the baked sponge. Like most chocolate cakes this one gets better a few days after baking. And, of course, it should be served with whipped cream.

Serves 10–12

200g dark chocolate (about 70 per cent cocoa solids), finely chopped
150g unsalted butter, softened
150g caster sugar
5 eggs plus 1 egg white, at room temperature
A good pinch of salt
150g plain flour
½ tsp baking powder

For the apricot glaze
5 tbsp apricot conserve or high fruit content jam

1 tsp lemon juice
1 tbsp water

For the chocolate covering
125ml double cream
175g dark chocolate (about 70 per cent cocoa solids), finely chopped
A little melted milk chocolate for piping (optional)
Whipped cream to serve

Grease and base-line a 23cm springclip tin (see page 11). Preheat the oven to 170°C.

Gently melt the chopped chocolate in a heatproof bowl set over a pan of steaming hot but not boiling water; don't let the base of the bowl touch the water. Avoid stirring; just tilt the bowl and gently push any unmelted chocolate under the surface. Remove from the heat and leave to cool.

Put the butter into a mixing bowl and beat until creamy, with the consistency of mayonnaise, then gradually beat in half the sugar. Scrape down the sides of the bowl and beat for about 4 minutes until the mixture is light and fluffy. Scrape down the sides of the bowl from time to time to incorporate all the mixture.

Separate the eggs, putting the six whites into a spotlessly clean large mixing bowl with the salt.

Beat the yolks one at a time into the butter mixture, beating well after each addition. Gently stir the cooled chocolate into the yolk and butter mixture, then sift the flour and baking powder into the bowl and gently fold in using a large metal spoon.

Whisk the egg whites with an electric mixer until they stand in soft peaks, then whisk in the remaining sugar, a tablespoon at a time, to make a glossy stiff meringue. Fold into the chocolate mixture in three batches. When the mixture is combined, spoon it into the prepared tin and spread evenly.

Bake for 50–60 minutes or until a cocktail stick pushed into the centre of the cake comes out clean.

Put the tin on a wire rack, run a round-bladed knife around the inside of the tin to loosen the sponge, then leave to firm up for 5 minutes before carefully turning out. Leave to cool completely.

When ready to finish the cake, turn it upside down on a wire rack – the flat base will be easier to ice.

To make the apricot glaze: gently warm the apricot conserve or jam, lemon juice and water in a small pan, stirring and pressing down on any large pieces of fruit to make a smooth, thick glaze. Bring to the boil, then brush over the top and sides of the cake. Leave to cool on the wire rack.

To make the chocolate covering: heat the cream until almost boiling. Put the chopped chocolate into a heatproof bowl and pour the hot cream over it. Leave for 2–3 minutes until melted, then gently stir to make a smooth, glossy ganache icing. Put a plate under the rack to catch the drips, then pour the chocolate over the cake to cover the top and sides. Leave to firm up in a cool place (not the fridge). If you like, you can pipe the letter S on top with melted milk chocolate in a small icing bag.

Store in an airtight container in a cool place for a couple of days before cutting into small slices. Serve with whipped cream.

Devil's Food Cake

The first recorded recipe for a devilishly tempting dark and rich layered chocolate cake with a snowy marshmallow frosting was published in America in 1902 by Sarah Tyson Rorer. Soured cream plus bicarbonate of soda help to give the cake its soft and fluffy texture. The whisked egg white and sugar frosting can be left bright white or quickly browned with a kitchen blowtorch.

Serves 10–12

100g dark chocolate (about 70 per cent cocoa solids)
30g cocoa powder
175ml boiling water
125g unsalted butter, softened
175g light muscovado sugar
175g golden caster sugar
2 eggs, beaten
300g plain flour
125ml soured cream, at room temperature
1 tsp bicarbonate of soda

For the fudge filling
100ml milk

65g caster sugar
50g dark chocolate (about 70 per cent cocoa solids)
45g unsalted butter, softened
½ tsp vanilla extract
¼–½ tsp ground black pepper, to taste

For the marshmallow frosting
325g white caster sugar
2 egg whites, at room temperature
A good pinch of salt
1 tbsp maple syrup
1 tsp vanilla extract
100ml water

Grease and base-line three 20cm round deep sandwich tins (see page 11) and dust with cocoa powder. Preheat the oven to 180°C.

Chop the chocolate into evenly sized pieces and gently melt in a heatproof bowl set over a pan of steaming hot but not boiling water; don't let the base of the bowl touch the water. Remove the bowl from the heat, stir gently until smooth and then leave to cool.

Weigh the cocoa into another heatproof bowl, pour in the boiling water and stir or whisk until smooth. Set aside.

Put the butter and both sugars into a large mixing bowl or the bowl of a stand mixer fitted with the paddle beater and beat well until smooth and light, about 3 minutes. Gradually beat in the eggs, beating well after each addition.

On low speed gradually mix in the flour alternately with the soured cream. Stir the bicarbonate of soda into the cocoa liquid, then combine it with the melted chocolate and add to the bowl. Mix thoroughly and then divide the mixture equally between the three prepared tins (if necessary, bake in batches, wiping out and preparing the tins as before).

Bake for about 20–25 minutes or until firm and a cocktail stick pushed into the centre of the cakes comes out clean.

Leave to cool and firm up for about 5 minutes, then run a round-bladed knife around the inside of the tins to loosen the sponges and carefully turn out onto wire racks – the sponges will be fragile so handle carefully. Leave until cold.

Meanwhile, make the fudge filling: heat the milk with the sugar in a small pan, stirring until the sugar has dissolved. Bring to the boil and boil rapidly for 1 minute. Remove from the heat, then chop the chocolate into evenly sized pieces and stir in, followed by the butter, vanilla and black pepper to taste to make a smooth, glossy mixture. Leave until thick but still spreadable.

Put one sponge, crust side down, on a wire rack and spread with half of the fudge filling. Top with a second sponge and spread with the remaining filling. Put the third sponge on top, crust side uppermost.

To make the marshmallow frosting: put the sugar and egg whites into a large heatproof bowl. Set over a pan of gently simmering water and whisk using an electric mixer until frothy. Add the salt, maple syrup, vanilla and the water and whisk on high speed for 8 minutes. Remove the bowl from the heat and continue whisking for another 15–20 minutes until the frosting has cooled and become very thick and white. Use immediately to swirl over the top and sides of the cake to completely cover.

If you like, quickly toast to a light brown colour with a kitchen blowtorch. Leave until set and firm before cutting.

Sea Salt Caramel Sponge

A winning combination of three layers of sponge cake, sandwiched with a rich chocolate caramel filling and a thick, dark caramel frosting offset with a dash of sea salt flakes. A little salt nicely balances the sweetness, but you could use lightly salted butter for the caramel mixture and omit the sea salt flakes. This cake is best made a day before cutting.

Serves 10–12

250g unsalted butter, softened
275g golden caster sugar
4 eggs
300g self-raising flour
¼ tsp salt
1 tsp vanilla extract
75ml natural unsweetened yogurt
   (not Greek-style)

*For the chocolate caramel filling
and caramel frosting*
225g unsalted butter, at room
   temperature

450g dark muscovado sugar
175ml double cream
250g icing sugar, sifted
¼–½ tsp sea salt flakes, to taste
70g dark chocolate (about
   70 per cent cocoa solids), finely
   chopped

To decorate
About 30g dark chocolate
   (70 per cent cocoa solids),
   grated or curls

Grease and base-line three 20cm round deep sandwich tins (see page 11). Preheat the oven to 180°C.

Put the butter into a large mixing bowl and beat until creamy, then gradually beat in the sugar. Scrape down the sides of the bowl and beat thoroughly for about 4 minutes until the mixture is lighter in texture and colour.

125

Scrape down the sides of the bowl again and gradually beat in the eggs, beating well after each addition and adding a tablespoon of the flour with each of the last two additions of egg to prevent the mixture from splitting.

Sift the remaining flour and the salt into the bowl. Stir the vanilla extract into the yogurt, then add to the mixture. Carefully fold everything together using a large metal spoon, then divide the mixture equally between the three prepared tins and spread evenly (if necessary, bake in batches, wiping out and preparing the tins as before).

Bake for about 22–25 minutes until the sponges are golden and spring back when gently pressed in the centre. Run a round-bladed knife around the inside of each tin to loosen the sponges, then turn out onto a wire rack and leave to cool.

Meanwhile, make the caramel mixture: put 175g of the butter into a heavy-based saucepan with the muscovado sugar and the cream. Heat gently, stirring with a wooden spoon, until melted and smooth. Turn up the heat and bring the mixture to the boil, stirring constantly. Once it has boiled, reduce the heat again and leave the mixture to simmer gently for 5 minutes, stirring constantly so that the mixture doesn't catch on the bottom of the pan.

Carefully pour the mixture into a heatproof bowl or the bowl of a stand mixer and immediately start to beat with the paddle beater or a wooden spoon; slowly beat in the icing sugar. Once all the sugar has been incorporated, beat on low speed for about 10 minutes or until the mixture is barely warm, and light in texture. Then beat in the remaining butter (if the mixture is too warm the butter will melt) and finally add sea salt flakes to taste. Cover and leave at room temperature.

Put the chopped chocolate into a heatproof bowl and gently melt over a pan of steaming hot but not boiling water; don't let the base of the bowl touch the water. Remove the bowl from the heat and stir gently until smooth, then leave to cool until just fluid. Weigh 250g of the caramel mixture and mix it into the melted chocolate. Leave to firm up until it becomes easy to spread (cover the remaining caramel).

Use the chocolate mixture to sandwich the three sponges, then put the cake on a wire rack set over a plate to catch the drips. Using an off-set palette knife, thickly spread the remaining caramel over the top and sides of the cake – if the mixture has become too firm to spread easily, gently warm it by setting the bowl over a pan of steaming water, stirring until it is the right consistency.

Decorate the top of the cake with grated chocolate or chocolate curls before the frosting has set.

Chocolate Cherry Roll (GF)

This richly flavoured, light-textured flourless sponge is really a soufflé mixture of eggs – the whites and yolks whisked separately – and melted dark chocolate. The filling is fresh cherries and whipped cream; you could also use raspberries or, for a winter treat, sweetened chestnut purée and rum.

Serves 10–12

175g dark chocolate (about 70 per cent cocoa solids)
6 eggs
A good pinch of salt
175g caster sugar
1 tbsp cocoa powder

For the filling
225ml double cream or plant-based whippable cream, well chilled
3 tbsp caster sugar
½ tsp vanilla extract

1–2 tsp kirsch, brandy or dark rum (optional)
300g fresh cherries or raspberries, or a 250g tin of crème de marrons (sweetened chestnut purée)

To finish
Icing sugar for dusting
Grated chocolate or chocolate curls or marrons glacés (optional)

Grease and line a 23 x 33cm Swiss roll tin (see page 11). Alternatively, fold a 27 x 37cm sheet of parchment-lined foil to make a 23 x 33 x 2cm case and place, foil side down, on a baking tray. Preheat the oven to 180°C.

Chop the chocolate into evenly sized pieces and put into a heatproof bowl. Set over a pan of steaming hot but not boiling water; don't let the base of the bowl touch the water. Leave to melt gently: avoid stirring – just tilt the bowl and gently press any unmelted chocolate under the surface. Remove the bowl from the pan and stir gently just until smooth. Set aside.

Separate the eggs, putting the whites and the salt into a spotlessly clean large mixing bowl or the bowl of a stand mixer, and the yolks into another mixing bowl. Using an electric mixer, whisk the whites until they form soft peaks. Whisk in 2 tablespoons of the sugar and keep whisking for a few seconds until the mixture forms stiff peaks. Set aside.

Add the remaining sugar to the egg yolks and whisk (no need to wash the whisk) for about 3–4 minutes until very thick and mousse-like and the mixture falls in a distinct ribbon-like trail when the whisk is lifted out of the mixture.

Add the cooled chocolate to the yolk mixture and gently fold in using a large metal spoon. Add a quarter of the stiff egg whites and stir in to loosen the mixture. Carefully fold in the remaining egg whites in three batches. Sift the cocoa powder on top and carefully fold in.

Transfer the mixture to the prepared tin, making sure the corners are neatly filled to give the final cake a good shape.

Bake for about 15–20 minutes until well risen and the top feels just firm when gently pressed.

Remove from the oven and put the tin on a wire rack (or slide the foil case onto the rack from the baking tray). If using a Swiss roll tin, gently run a round-bladed knife around the inside of the tin to loosen the sponge. Leave the sponge to cool in the tin or case – it will probably shrink.

Meanwhile, make the filling: whip the chilled cream with the sugar and vanilla until it stands in soft peaks. Whisk in a splash of kirsch, if liked, to go with cherries or raspberries, or brandy or dark rum if using chestnut purée.

Set aside a few of the best-looking cherries (or raspberries) and about 3 tablespoons of the whipped cream for the decoration, then stone and halve the remaining cherries. Stir the halved cherries (or the remaining raspberries or all the chestnut purée) into the rest of the whipped cream.

Lightly dust a large sheet of baking paper with icing sugar. Flip out the sponge onto the paper, then remove the tin and peel off the lining paper. Using a large sharp knife, make a shallow cut along one short end of the sponge, about 2cm in from the edge. Gently spread the whipped cream mixture over the sponge, leaving a 2cm border all around. Gently fold the cut edge over, then roll up the sponge fairly tightly, using the sugar-dusted paper to help you pull the roll into a neat shape with the join underneath – the roll will crack but the paper will hold it together. Cover and place in the fridge to firm up for at least an hour or overnight.

When ready to serve, neatly trim the ragged ends and slide the roll onto a serving plate. To decorate, dust with more icing sugar or grated chocolate, then neatly spoon or pipe the reserved cream along the top and finish with the reserved fruit, or with chocolate curls or marrons glacés.

Small Cakes

These little cakes are, by and large, defined by their speed and simplicity. Rock Cakes (page 137) and Welsh Cakes (page 142) are grander and richer than scones, but are just as quick to make and cook and don't need to be spread with butter.

Dainty sponge cakes can be assembled and baked faster than their larger cousins. Little shell-shaped Madeleines (page 150), invented by pastry cook Madeleine Paulmier in Commercy, France, in the eighteenth century, taste rich and buttery and look pretty enough not to need decoration or icing. Fairy cakes, which are usually iced, are delicate versions of a simple sponge cake.

Brownies have been a favourite American treat since the nineteenth century and get their name thanks to copious amounts of dark chocolate or cocoa. The more modern blondies offer a different look, with their combination of good-quality white chocolate and raspberries.

Rock cakes (or rock buns) first appeared as Imperials – rather solid fruit buns made from plain flour, currants and candied peel – in Eliza Acton's *Modern Cookery for Private Families* published in 1845. By the 1880s they were lighter, more crumbly (with the help of baking powder), often flavoured with lemon zest or brandy and included raisins and spices such as nutmeg and mace. They have evolved, with a richer and spicier mixture to add to the now iconic rock-like appearance.

Tiffin (GF)

No baking is necessary for this immensely popular melt-and-mix chocolate fridge cake. It appears to have originated in Troon in Scotland at the beginning of the twentieth century, and it is still made there with the addition of plenty of raisins. An extravagant version, coated in chocolate ganache icing, was created by Buckingham Palace chefs as one of the two wedding cakes to celebrate the marriage of Prince William and Catherine Middleton (now Prince and Princess of Wales) in 2011. This indulgent recipe includes chunks of stem ginger preserved in syrup, and bright pistachios.

Makes 25 squares

100g shelled unsalted pistachios
225g dark chocolate (about 70 per cent cocoa solids)
110g unsalted butter, diced
2 tbsp golden syrup
1 tbsp ginger syrup from the jar
65g drained stem ginger (3–4 lumps), chopped

225g petit beurre, rich tea or digestive biscuits (gluten-free or original)
Sea salt flakes for sprinkling (optional)

Oil a 20cm square cake tin and line with parchment-lined foil or baking paper.

Tip the pistachios into a small pan and add cold water to just cover. Bring to the boil over a medium-low heat. Drain thoroughly in a sieve or colander, then tip the nuts onto a clean tea towel and gently rub off the papery brown skins.

The next step is optional: preheat the oven to 180°C. Put the pistachios into an ovenproof dish and lightly toast in the oven for about 7 minutes – this adds to their flavour and crunchy texture. Leave to cool (you won't need the oven again).

Break up the chocolate into evenly sized pieces and put into a heatproof bowl large enough to hold all the ingredients. Add the butter, golden syrup and ginger syrup and set the bowl over a pan of steaming hot but not boiling water; don't let the base of the bowl touch the water. Leave to melt gently, stirring now and then with a wooden spoon.

Once the mixture is smooth, remove the bowl from the pan. Stir in the ginger. Set aside about 20g of the best-looking pistachios, then roughly chop the rest and stir in.

Using your hands – rather than a food processor or rolling pin – chop the biscuits into pieces about the size of your thumb nail; they don't need to be evenly sized or neat, but you don't want a lot of crumbs either. Add to the bowl and mix in thoroughly so that the biscuits are coated in the chocolate mixture.

Transfer to the prepared tin and spread evenly – there is no need to compress the mixture or neaten the surface. Scatter with the reserved pistachios and a sprinkling of sea salt flakes, if using.

Cover the tin and chill until set – at least 3 hours, or overnight.

Carefully turn out, using the lining paper to help, then cut into 25 squares.

Spicy Rock Cakes

Craggy-looking rock cakes were among the recipes collected by Mrs Beeton and published in her *Book of Household Management* in 1861. During the Second World War, when rationing made home baking an exercise in logistics, the Ministry of Food was quick to promote the humble rock cake into treat status. The *Harry Potter* character Hagrid has played a part in bringing rock cakes to the attention of younger bakers after he baked some for Harry and his friends.

Makes 12

225g white spelt flour or plain flour
2 tsp baking powder
¼ tsp salt
½ tsp ground mixed spice
½ tsp ground cinnamon
90g unsalted butter, chilled and diced
80g golden caster sugar

100g dried mixed fruit and peel or luxury dried fruit mix (with diced apricots, cranberries, raisins, etc.)
1 egg, at room temperature
2 tbsp milk or single cream
1 tbsp sugar for sprinkling: pearl, demerara or golden caster

Grease a baking tray. Preheat the oven to 200°C.

Sift the flour, baking powder, salt, mixed spice and ground cinnamon into a mixing bowl. Add the diced butter and toss it briefly in the flour to coat the pieces. Using your fingertips, rub the butter into the flour until the mixture looks like coarse breadcrumbs.

Mix in the sugar and dried fruit using a wooden spoon. Lightly beat the egg with the milk or cream, until just combined. Gradually stir into the flour and fruit mixture until it just comes together to make a very firm, stiff dough. If there are dry crumbs in the base of the bowl and the dough won't stick together, add more milk or cream, a teaspoon at a time – take care with this as the cakes will spread out in the oven if the dough is too wet.

Divide the dough evenly into 12 heaped, peaky mounds, well spaced, on the prepared tray. Sprinkle with sugar, then bake for 12–15 minutes until a good golden brown and just firm to touch.

Transfer to a wire rack and leave to cool until just warm before eating. Best eaten on the day of baking or the next day.

Butterfly Fairy Cakes

Miniature vanilla sponge cakes, made the all-in-one way and baked in paper cases, are a favourite treat whatever your age. After baking, a thin disc of sponge is cut from the top of each cake and halved to form wings, ready to press into a swirl of butter icing and finish with a fresh berry.

Makes 12

115g unsalted butter, softened
115g caster sugar
2 eggs, beaten
2 tsp milk
½ tsp vanilla extract
115g self-raising flour
A pinch of salt
¼ tsp baking powder

To decorate
65g unsalted butter, softened
200g icing sugar, plus extra for dusting
2 tbsp milk
½ tsp vanilla extract or the finely grated zest of 1 unwaxed lemon
12 fresh berries (strawberries, raspberries, dessert blackberries or a mixture)

Place 12 paper fairy cake cases in a bun tray or mince pie tray. Preheat the oven to 200°C.

Put the butter and sugar into a mixing bowl or the bowl of a stand mixer. Combine the eggs with the milk and vanilla and add to the bowl. Sift the flour, salt and baking powder into the bowl and then beat with a wooden spoon or electric mixer: start slowly and then increase the speed once all the ingredients are incorporated. Scrape down the sides of the bowl and continue beating for about 3 minutes or until the mixture is very light and smooth.

Spoon the mixture into the paper cases. Put the tray into the oven and immediately reduce the oven temperature to 180°C. Bake for about 12–15 minutes until the cakes are golden and springy when gently pressed in the centre.

Carefully transfer the fairy cakes to a wire rack and leave to cool.

Meanwhile, make the butter icing for the decoration: put the butter into a mixing bowl and beat until creamy, with the consistency of mayonnaise. Sift the icing sugar into the bowl, add the milk and the vanilla or lemon zest and beat until very smooth and thick: start slowly to avoid a mess.

To assemble the butterfly cakes: using a sharp knife, such as a serrated tomato knife, slice a thin disc about 4cm across from the top of each fairy cake. Cut each disc in half to make two semi-circles. Spoon a large dollop of butter icing over the exposed sponge of each fairy cake (you can also pipe swirls with a piping bag fitted with a star tube). Gently press the straight edge of each semi-circle into the soft icing at an angle to resemble the wings of a butterfly. Set a berry in the centre of each cake, then dust with icing sugar.

Wholewheat Blueberry Muffins

Packed with juicy berries and quick to prepare. Yogurt gives these nutritious muffins a moist and light texture.

Makes 12

275g wholemeal plain flour
¼ tsp salt
2 tsp baking powder
½ tsp bicarbonate of soda
125g demerara sugar
Finely grated zest of 1 unwaxed
   lemon plus 1 tbsp juice
135g fresh (or frozen) blueberries

65g unsalted butter, melted
130ml natural unsweetened yogurt
   (not Greek-style)
2 eggs

To finish
2 tbsp demerara sugar or granola

Line a 12-hole cupcake or muffin tray with paper cases. Preheat the oven to 220°C.

Weigh the flour into a large mixing bowl and stir in the salt, baking powder, bicarbonate of soda, sugar, grated lemon zest (not the juice) and blueberries.

Stir the melted butter into the yogurt, then add the eggs and mix thoroughly. Stir in the lemon juice, then add to the dry ingredients and mix until just combined.

Spoon the mixture into the paper cases, sprinkle with sugar or granola and bake for 10 minutes. Reduce the oven temperature to 200°C and bake for a further 8–10 minutes until golden and firm to the touch.

Transfer to a wire rack and leave to cool before eating just warm or at room temperature.

Welsh Cakes

Welsh cakes, halfway between a pancake and a scone, are cooked on a heavy cast-iron griddle, either set over an open fire or on the stove. The mixture is often spooned directly onto the clean hot plate of a solid-fuel range cooker, though this requires intimate knowledge of the hot spots.

Fresh Welsh cakes, warm from the griddle, are an essential taste of Wales. One scenic spot to enjoy this classic treat is the National Trust café at Powis Castle, Welshpool – a medieval fortress, remodelled in seventeenth-century style, with Italianate terraces that are considered some of the finest in Europe.

Makes about 18

225g self-raising flour, plus extra
    for dusting
A large pinch of ground mixed
    spice
¼ tsp salt
100g unsalted butter, chilled and
    diced

70g caster sugar, plus extra for
    sprinkling
25g currants
1 egg, beaten with 1 tbsp milk

Sift the flour, spice and salt into a mixing bowl. Add the butter and rub in using your fingertips until the mixture looks like fine crumbs. Stir in the sugar and currants and then, using a round-bladed knife, mix in enough of the egg and milk mixture to make a soft but not sticky dough. If the dough is dry, add a little more milk.

Turn the dough out onto a lightly floured worktop and roll out to about 1.5cm thick, then cut into rounds using a 5–6cm round fluted cutter.

Gather up the trimmings, re-roll the dough and cut more rounds.

Heat a griddle or heavy frying pan. If you think it necessary, grease it with a smear of butter on a piece of kitchen paper, but Welsh cakes should not be fried. Cook the cakes in batches until puffed up and a good golden brown – about 2–3 minutes on each side. Lift out, sprinkle with sugar and eat while they're warm.

Apricot Marzipan Squares

An easy recipe using fresh apricots to make a glamorous cake. It is simply put together using the rubbed-in method. Adding small cubes of marzipan to the fruit topping adds a special touch to these rather elegant squares.

Makes 16

300g stoneground white spelt flour
   (plus 1 tbsp baking powder) or
   300g self-raising flour
A good pinch of salt
150g unsalted butter, chilled and
   diced
100g golden caster sugar
125g sultanas
2 eggs

½ tsp vanilla extract
150ml milk
4 just-ripe fresh apricots
100g marzipan, cut into 1cm cubes

To finish
2 tbsp apricot conserve
1 tbsp hot water
2 tbsp flaked almonds

Grease and base-line a 20cm square cake tin (see page 11). Preheat the oven to 180°C.

Sift the flour, baking powder (if using) and salt into a mixing bowl. Add the butter and toss it in the flour until lightly coated. Using your fingertips, rub the butter and flour together until the mixture looks like fine breadcrumbs.

Stir in the sugar and sultanas. Beat the eggs with the vanilla and milk, add to the bowl and mix everything together with a wooden spoon to make a stiff mixture that drops off the spoon with a shake of the wrist.

Transfer the mixture to the prepared tin and spread evenly. Halve the apricots and remove the stones, then cut each half in two to make 16 wedges. Arrange on top of the cake, skin side up, then scatter the marzipan between the wedges.

Bake for 40–45 minutes or until a cocktail stick pushed into the centre comes out clean.

Stand the tin on a wire rack. Gently warm the apricot conserve with the water until it is just runny, then carefully brush and dab it over the warm cake to give a glossy, sticky glaze. Sprinkle with the flaked almonds, then leave to cool before removing from the tin and cutting into squares.

Double Chocolate Brownies

This is very similar to a brownie recipe that appeared in an American newspaper in the 1950s as part of an article on favourite church bakes. The sugar from the original recipe has been greatly reduced, and the quality of the chocolate increased, to suit current tastes, but the insistence on slight underbaking to retain a soft, melting texture remains.

You can personalise this recipe by adding a teaspoon of instant coffee dissolved in a tablespoon of boiling water at the end, along with the chocolate, or by adding a few more sea salt flakes to the top before baking, or by omitting the nuts.

Makes 25

180g dark chocolate (about 70 per cent cocoa solids)
90g unsalted butter, softened
240g caster sugar
4 eggs
1 tsp vanilla extract

55g plain flour
55g cocoa powder
¼ tsp sea salt flakes
100g walnut pieces (optional)
Icing sugar for dusting

Grease and base-line a 20cm square cake tin (see page 11). Preheat the oven to 170°C.

Chop the chocolate into evenly sized pieces and put into a heatproof bowl. Set over a pan of steaming hot but not boiling water; don't let the base of the bowl touch the water. Leave to melt slowly, then remove the bowl from the pan and stir gently a couple of times until smooth. Leave to cool.

Put the butter and sugar into a mixing bowl or the bowl of a stand mixer and beat well until thoroughly combined.

Beat the eggs with the vanilla in a separate bowl, then gradually beat into the butter and sugar mixture, beating well after each addition. Sift the flour and cocoa into the bowl and stir in, then add the salt, melted chocolate and walnuts, if using, and stir well. Transfer to the prepared tin and spread evenly.

Bake for about 25 minutes or until almost firm to the touch: a cocktail stick pushed into the centre will come out with sticky mixture attached (if it comes out clean the brownies will be dry).

Put the tin on a wire rack and leave until cold. If possible, leave overnight before dusting with icing sugar and cutting into 25 squares.

White Chocolate Blondies

Made in much the same way as brownies, but with top-quality white chocolate (look out for bars with 30 per cent cocoa solids) and decorated with fresh raspberries or blackberries to balance the richness.

Makes 25

165g white chocolate (about
    30 per cent cocoa solids)
135g unsalted butter, diced
2 eggs
A good pinch of salt
100g golden caster sugar

½ tsp vanilla extract
135g self-raising flour
100g fresh raspberries or dessert
    blackberries
Icing sugar for dusting

Grease and base-line a 20cm square cake tin (see page 11). Preheat the oven to 180°C.

Break up 100g of the chocolate and put into a heatproof bowl. Add the butter and set over a pan of steaming hot but not boiling water; don't let the base of the bowl touch the water. Leave to melt gently: avoid stirring – just tilt the bowl and gently press any unmelted chocolate under the surface. Remove the bowl from the pan, stir gently to just combine, then leave to cool.

Break the eggs into a mixing bowl or the bowl of a stand mixer, add the salt and whisk with an electric whisker until frothy. Add the sugar and vanilla and whisk on high speed for about 3 minutes until very thick and mousse-like. Whisk in the chocolate and butter mixture on low speed.

Sift the flour into the bowl and gently fold in using a large metal spoon.

Roughly chop the remaining chocolate into pieces about the size of your little fingernail and gently mix in. Transfer the mixture to the prepared tin and spread evenly.

Arrange the berries on top of the mixture, then bake for about 25–30 minutes or until just firm and a cocktail stick pushed into the centre comes out clean.

Put the tin on a wire rack and leave to cool. Remove from the tin and cut into 25 squares. Dust with icing sugar just before serving.

Chocolate Madeleines

Made from a light whisked sponge mixture with cocoa and honey for plenty of flavour, these elegant little cakes are baked in special shell-shaped madeleine moulds. These come in various sizes, so you may need to bake in batches. If buying new, the flexible or non-stick types work best, but it is still worth brushing them with a couple of thin layers of melted butter before filling with the chilled mixture.

Makes about 15

100g unsalted butter, plus extra for greasing
2 eggs
60g caster sugar
25g well-flavoured honey
70g plain flour

20g cocoa powder
A good pinch of salt
¼ tsp baking powder
50g ground almonds
Icing sugar for dusting

Brush your madeleine moulds with melted butter, chill until set, then repeat.

Melt the butter in a small pan over a low heat, then set aside to cool.

Break the eggs into a large mixing bowl or the bowl of a stand mixer and whisk for a minute on low speed, just until frothy. Add the sugar and honey and whisk on medium speed until combined, and then on high speed for 3–4 minutes until the mixture is very thick and mousse-like and falls in a distinct ribbon-like trail when the whisk is lifted out of the mixture.

Sift the flour, cocoa, salt, baking powder and almonds into the bowl and gently fold everything together using a large metal spoon. Pour in the cooled melted butter and fold in until just combined. Cover the bowl and chill until firm – about 1 hour.

When ready to bake, preheat the oven to 200°C.

Scoop the mixture into the prepared moulds so that each is about three-quarters full, then bake for about 8–12 minutes or until the sponge keeps its shape when gently pressed (the time will depend on the size and type of mould).

Turn out onto a wire rack and leave to cool, then dust with icing sugar. If baking in batches, wipe out the moulds and then brush again with butter between each bake.

Rhubarb and Almond Cake

Packwood House in Warwickshire, now in the care of the National Trust, was described by a guest in the 1930s as a 'house to dream of, a garden to dream in'. The eighteenth-century kitchen garden has been restored to recreate the once-vital part of the Fetherston family's self-sufficient home. The café at Packwood makes full use of the amazing home-grown produce, including an abundance of rhubarb, starting in early spring with tender pink 'forced' stalks and continuing into summer. Their recipe is like a rhubarb Bakewell tart, with plenty of fruit to match the richly moist almond layers.

Makes 12 pieces

275g trimmed young, tender spring rhubarb, rinsed
1 tbsp caster sugar, or to taste

For the almond mixture
150g unsalted butter, softened
150g caster sugar
2 eggs, beaten

100g self-raising flour
200g ground almonds
1 tsp baking powder
A good pinch of salt

To finish
2 tbsp flaked almonds
Icing sugar for dusting

Grease and base-line a 20cm square shallow cake tin (see page 11). Preheat the oven to 180°C.

Cut the rhubarb into chunks about 2–3cm long. Put into a bowl, add the caster sugar and mix well. Set aside.

To make the almond mixture: beat the butter and sugar together in a mixing bowl until the mixture is very light and creamy. Scrape down the sides of the bowl and gradually beat in the eggs, beating well after each addition and adding a tablespoon of the flour with each of the last two additions to prevent the mixture from splitting. Sift the remaining flour, the ground almonds, baking powder and salt into the bowl and carefully mix in using a large metal spoon or spatula – the mixture will feel a bit stiff.

Spoon half of the mixture into the prepared tin and spread evenly. Arrange half of the rhubarb pieces on top, then gently spoon the remaining almond mixture over them and carefully spread it out to completely cover the fruit and reach the sides of the tin. Arrange the remaining rhubarb on top and scatter over the flaked almonds. Cover the tin with foil and bake for 40 minutes.

Remove the foil and bake for a further 25–30 minutes until golden brown and the centre feels just firm when gently pressed.

Put the tin on a wire rack and leave to cool before turning out. Dust with icing sugar and cut into 12 pieces.

Little Chelsea Buns

The Chelsea Bun House, situated in London's Pimlico district, was famous from the early 1700s until 1839 (when it was demolished) for sweet, sticky fruit buns so good that even King George III queued to buy them. A contemporary poet described them as tasting of honey, and being very light and sweet: 'Fragrant as honey and sweeter in taste! As flaky and white as if baked by the light, As the flesh of an infant soft, doughy and slight.'

Makes 24

185ml milk
50g unsalted butter
450g strong white bread flour
5g salt
2 tbsp light muscovado sugar
7g sachet easy-blend dried yeast
1 egg, at room temperature, beaten

For the filling
50g unsalted butter, melted
50g light muscovado sugar
125g dried mixed fruit

For the sticky glaze
3 tbsp milk
3 tbsp honey
2 tbsp light muscovado sugar

Thoroughly grease a baking tin or roasting tin about 30 x 22cm and line with greaseproof paper.

Gently warm the milk with the butter until the butter has melted – the mixture should feel comfortable to dip a finger into. Set aside for a minute.

Combine the flour, salt, sugar and dried yeast in a large bowl and make a well in the centre. Pour the milk mixture and the beaten

egg into the well and gradually work the flour into the liquids with your hand to make a slightly soft dough: if the mixture feels stiff or there are dry crumbs, work in a little more milk, a tablespoon at a time; if the dough sticks to the sides of the bowl work in a little more flour.

Turn out the dough onto a lightly floured worktop and knead it thoroughly for about 10 minutes until very pliable and smooth (you can also mix and knead the dough in a stand mixer fitted with a dough hook, kneading for 4 minutes on low speed). Return the dough to a clean, lightly oiled bowl, cover tightly and leave in a warm place until doubled in size – about 1–1½ hours.

Turn out the dough onto a lightly floured worktop and roll out to a rectangle about 60 x 20cm. Brush with the melted butter and then sprinkle with the sugar, followed by the dried fruit. Roll up the dough like a Swiss roll, starting from one long side. Pinch the seam to seal the dough roll.

Using a large sharp knife, cut the roll into 24 equal slices. Arrange the slices cut side up in the prepared tin so that they just touch. Lightly cover the tin and leave to rise as before until almost doubled in size – about 20 minutes. Meanwhile, preheat the oven to 200°C.

Uncover the tin and bake the buns for 20–30 minutes until golden brown – if the fruit starts to burn, cover the top of the tin loosely with greaseproof paper or foil.

Meanwhile, make the sticky glaze: gently warm the milk with the honey and sugar, stirring until dissolved, smooth and sticky. As soon as the buns are cooked, brush them with the warm glaze. Leave to cool, then gently remove from the tin and pull the buns apart.

Index

Note: page numbers in **bold** refer to illustrations.

Acknowledgements

I would like to thank: the National Trust for their help and for providing recipes from their properties; Peter Taylor and David Salmo at HarperCollins, and Maggie Ramsay for her thorough editing; Louise Morgan for her wonderful artwork; my dear friend and agent Barbara Levy; my husband, Prof Alan Hertz, who helped with the cake eating and fact-finding (all errors are mine); Daniel and Stevie Hertz, cake lovers both.

The book is dedicated to the Silver Swimmers at POTP who ate all the cakes, and to Mimi who made the coffee.